A BURDEN SHARED

P U B L I S H E R S
BOX 3566 • GRAND RAPIDS, MI 49501

*PUBLISHING BOOKS THAT FEED
THE SOUL WITH THE WORD OF GOD.*

A BURDEN SHARED

DAVID ROPER

A Burden Shared
Copyright © 1991 by David Roper
Discovery House Publishers is affiliated with Radio Bible Class
Grand Rapids, Michigan.
Discovery House books are distributed to the trade by
Thomas Nelson Publishers, Nashville, Tennessee 37214.

Unless indicated otherwise, Scripture is taken from the
HOLY BIBLE, NEW INTERNATIONAL VERSION.
Copyright © 1973, 1978, 1984 International Bible Society.
Used by permission of Zondervan Bible Publishers.

Library of Congress Cataloging-in-Publication Data

Roper, David, 1933–
    A burden shared / David Roper
        p.   cm.
    ISBN 0-929239-40-7
    1. Clergy—Religious life—Meditations. 2. Clergy—Office—
    Meditations. 3. Devotional calendars. I. Title
    BV4011.6.R67   1991   91-11617
    242'.692—dc20   CIP

Printed in the United States of America
91 92 93 94 95 / CH / 10 9 8 7 6 5 4 3 2

CONTENTS

DEDICATION

A Burden Shared developed out of my love for pastors, especially the back-country and rural pastors of Idaho. Many of them feel ill-equipped for their task. Most of them are under-paid, under-appreciated, over-worked, and often burdened with busy-work unrelated to the task of the ministry.

Few understand their plight. Most of these shepherds live in very harsh environments—cold weather, few amenities, and little social life or Christian fellowship. It's a struggle just to survive. But a harsher environment still is the spiritual climate of some of these communities. There is sometimes terrible spiritual coldness and a harshness and cruelty that withers the soul.

I'm an Idahoan by call and a flyfisher by choice—a happy coincidence where call and choice coincide—and in my travels around the state looking for rivers and streams I keep running into these dear folks. They are truly significant. Francis Schaefer was right: there are no little people and there are no little places.

My heart goes out to those who labor in obscure ministries like these. And it is to these hardy saints that I dedicate this book.

INTRODUCTION

As I watch my friends in ministry, I note an odd inconsistency: Most of them ardently believe in what they're doing, yet many are utterly discouraged. They find themselves much too busy, and, what may be worse, their busyness seems barren. Hence their disillusionment.

One of the problems is that our training (if we received any) may not have fully prepared us for the work to which we've been called. We've acquired a few tools and some skill to proceed with our task, but, when we get around to working with people, we sometimes find ourselves laboring on without some of the basic stuff of which the work is made, trying to make bricks without straw.

Getting the basics down, as any coach will tell you, is the name of the game. Yet we don't think much about the fundamentals because we're either too busy to think about them, or we assume we know what they are—an error akin to the old fallacy of believing you know the answer to a question before it's asked. The truth is that few ever ask about the fundamentals.

So we soldier on—getting busier, running in our own version of the fast lane, increasing our pace and our blood pressure, rushing to our own destruction like the Gadarene swine. Our densely-packed lives lead us to respond like the Mad Hatter, who, when he was told that the inhabitants of Alice's world had to run very fast to get anywhere, replied, "A very odd world. Here one must run very fast to stay in the same place." Equally apropos is the sentiment on a plaque that used to hang over my mother's desk: "The hurrier I go, the behinder I get." In the end, despite our zeal, we wear down, our expectations fade, and we consider bailing out. Nothing quite dispells the myth of ministry like being in it.

And so, as I think of my work and ponder ways to help others with theirs, my question has become one of basics: What are the parameters—the fixed reference points? What are the principles that apply everywhere, regardless of time and place? All too often, what works in one situation won't work in another, and if we try to force-fit an inappropriate solution, we can do a lot of harm.

Programs and procedures vary from place to place, but principles remain constant. They can be transferred from one situation to another. Hence my search for the fundamentals. I know they must come from God rather than from my own background and tradition because often my own experience doesn't apply. The safest course is to find a pattern in the Word. As George MacDonald said, "The design of God is always other and better than the designs of man." It's my hope that these essays reflect something of that Grand Design.

If there's any wisdom in my ministry, it comes from many sources, but mostly from my companion and co-laborer, Carolyn, who for the past thirty-four years has shared my life and work and helped me sort out truth from error. She is one of God's faithful servants—now the Minister of Women's Ministries at Cole Community Church—and one of my mentors; she is my Deborah, under whose palm tree and at whose feet I sit. The words in these writings may be mine, but the best ideas are hers.

What I offer are mere thoughts—ideas about serving others, in no particular order, most of which were originally written for workers that I know. This is not a how-to-do-ministry book. It's rather a set of musings about some things I'm learning after thirty years of ministry. Some of the essays are short simply because I had nothing more to say at the time. Others are longer; none are finished. In a year or two I'll probably want to rethink them, polish them up, fill them out. But for now I leave them as they are—an interim effort forced out of me by what I see around me in the church.

It is my hope that together we will learn and find rest in our labor. For, as our Lord assured us, His yoke was meant to be easy and His burden light.

David Roper
Boise, Idaho

HASTE THAT WASTES

Warm-up: Mark 1:9–12

You are my Son, whom I love;
with you I am well pleased
(Mark 1:11).

There's this fellow I know who's always in a hurry. I've forgotten his name, but I'll never forget his pace.

He's involved in everything that goes on down at the church: He's a chairman of committees, a leader of small groups, a teacher of small children, a whirlwind of pious fervor and activity. His life is full of bother and commotion. You can pick him out of any group: He's the one who wrings his hands every so often; the one with a foot of tongue hanging out. Just being around him makes me tired.

But his hectic pace doesn't seem right to me. In the first place, Jesus never behaved like that. He was never in a hurry! He had an infinite job to do and only three and one-half years in which to do it. And yet there's no trace of effort in His work. He never seemed hassled or harried. Even when people heaped on Him impossible demands, His manner was measured, deliberate.

Furthermore, Jesus didn't make it His practice to tell others to hurry. In fact, the only person He ever prodded into activity was Judas. "What you are about to do, do quickly," He said (John 13:27).

I keep wondering, then, why my friend imposes this tyrannical routine upon himself. No one is driving him; the pressure seems to come from within. Perhaps he has something yet to prove. To himself or to God.

I don't know why my friend works so hard, but I know why I'm inclined to do so. For some reason, much of my self-esteem is determined by what I do. That's why I get restless and unhappy when I'm inactive, and that's why I have to do more—far more than God or anyone else ever intended for me to do, far more than God designed my body to do. In fact, in my eccentric way, the busier I am the better I feel about myself. I feel best when I'm on the verge of exhaustion.

Jesus, on the other hand, didn't have to stay busy, because He knew that God's sons don't have to prove anything. Even when they're doing nothing that seems to be significant, they are significant because they're dear to the Father. Jesus knew, and He teaches us to know, that our self-identity doesn't arise from what we do but from what we are—fully accepted and beloved children of God.

Once after Jesus' disciples returned from a mission and excitedly reported their success, He countered with the mild rebuke: "Do not rejoice that the spirits submit to you, but rejoice that your names are written in heaven" (Luke 10:20). The disciples felt good about themselves because they had done well. It was far better, Jesus observed, to get one's joy from the knowledge that we're special to God, that He knows our names and has them in His book!

The Bible everywhere teaches that God is underwhelmed by our best efforts and unimpressed with our most spectacular achievements. It's not what we do for Him that matters nor should it matter much to us. What matters most is what we are to Him.

The Father's words at Jesus' baptism are significant: "You are my Son, whom I love; with you I am well pleased" (Mark 1:11). What had Jesus done? What had He accomplished that merited such unqualified acceptance and admiration? He hadn't yet preached a sermon, delivered a sinner, or done any of His so-called "mighty deeds." He had, in fact, done nothing we normally associate with greatness.

He was pleasing to the Father merely because He was God's beloved Son. That's all.

And what's true of Him is true of us as well. Our Father delights in us (Ps. 18:19). He loves us whether we're worthy or unworthy; whether we're faithful or unfaithful. He loves us without boundary or limit. No matter what we do or leave undone He cannot stop loving us.

And so, we don't have to do anything to feel good about ourselves; we don't always have to be in a hurry. We can run in the slow lane. We can make time for the peace of God to rule our hearts and minds. We can take a part of each day or a portion of each week to be alone with Him. We can take a day off. We can take a vacation. We can miss a meeting or two. We can leave some tasks undone at the end of each day and go home. We can take time to talk and take long walks with our spouses and children. We can hunt, fish, and golf with our friends.

Philip Melanchthon and Martin Luther were once deciding on the day's agenda. Melanchthon said,

"Martin, this day we will discuss the governance of the universe." To which Luther replied, "This day you and I will go fishing and leave governance of the universe to God."

As old "Satchel" Paige used to say, when we work we can work hard, but when we sit, we can sit loose. We don't have to be dogged and driven by our work. We don't have to prove anything, because we don't have anything left to prove. We're already approved. The good news is that God uplifts and accepts you and me.

INCOMPETENCE

Warm-up: 2 Corinthians 3:1–4:18

Not that we are competent in our-
selves to claim anything . . . ,
but our competence comes from God.
He has made us competent as ministers
of a new covenant . . . (2 Cor. 3:5–6).

Some things stick like cockleburs to one's mind. I can't forget a conversation early in my ministry when I sought out an older friend and confessed my incompetence to him. I knew deep down that I had exhausted my resources; I had nothing left to give. "I'm inadequate," I lamented.

"Indeed you are m'boy," he agreed, with a twinkle in his eyes, "and so am I, and it's good that we know it. Some people labor all their lives, never knowing that they don't have what it takes."

As Popeye says, "I yam what I yam," and what I "yam" is incompetent; my limitations are limitless. And there's a "holy host of others standing 'round me." Human limitation is a fact of life, a hard truth that makes life easier when we accept it. "We're all ordinary people," said G. K. Chesterton, "and it's the extraordinary people who know it."

Paul agreed. He said, "We have this treasure [our ministry] in *jars of clay* [our humanity] to show that this all-surpassing power is from God and not from us"

(2 Cor. 4:7, emphasis added). Unaided humanity is useless; "the flesh [human effort] counts for nothing" (John. 6:63). If anything is to be done, God must do it. The people who work the works of God are those who realize their utter unfitness and overwhelming inadequacy to do the task. "We are weak in Him," is not a platitude but a certainty. It irks us to think of ourselves so useless, but therein lies our strength.

The problem with many of us is that we're much too gifted; we're perilously adequate. And so we go on our way, believing in ourselves and our own power and personality, relying on our own strength and show. But our self-confidence is our stumbling block. We're so good at what we do we're no good at all. So God must thwart our energy at its source.

He wears down our noble resolve through the frustrations of life and He wrings out of us every vestige of self-confidence by disappointment and defeat. He allows our cherished projects to founder; the wheels fall off our cleverly contrived programs; our dreams go belly up. He tutors us through our flops and failures until we learn that most precious of all God's premises: *We can't!*

And then, when "can-do" can't, He shows us that *He can*, and therefore *we can*. ("I can't" then becomes blasphemy.) The demands that have been placed on us are now demands on Him; the pressures and problems are His! Then, we can say with the apostle, "We are hard pressed on every side, but not crushed; perplexed, but not in despair; persecuted, but not abandoned; struck down, but not destroyed" (2 Cor. 4:8–9).

There are still those stalemates and stand-offs that frustrate us, but they're honorably resolved in His time.

We're sometimes confused and uncertain, not knowing what to do or say, but when we have to know, we know! We're still hounded and harassed by people, principalities, and powers, but we're shadowed and sheltered under His wings. We get down now and then, but we're never out! We can, in fact, do all things that must be done, through the One who strengthens us. God's activity through our fragile humanity is our great assurance!

We should then, as George MacDonald said, "confess ourselves poor creatures, for that is the beginning of being great men and great women. To persuade ourselves that we are something when we are nothing is terrible loss; to confess that we are nothing is to lay the foundation of being something."

MERE MINISTRY

Warm-up: Acts 20:17–21

*You know how I lived the whole
time I was with you, from the first
day I came into the province
of Asia. I served the Lord with great
humility and with tears. . . .
I have not hesitated to preach anything that would be helpful to you
but have taught you publicly and
from house to house (Acts 20:18–20).*

I am often asked, "What on earth should I be doing?" I
hear it from pastors, leaders, and Christian workers of
all kinds. It's a good question.

Certainly, we're not looking for more to do. We're
busy people. We have calls to make, books to read,
meetings to attend, messages to prepare. Our calendars
are filled with appointments, our days are consumed
with engagements, our minds are crammed with
projects.

And so we move through the day in our distracted
way, assuming that our compulsions are mandates from
God. We accept the tributes that are given to busy
people, but when we have time to evaluate what we're
doing, it occurs to us that what we're doing isn't worth
doing at all, at least in terms of eternal significance.

On the other hand, Paul seemed to know exactly
what he was doing and believed that what he was doing

was thoroughly worthwhile. He summarized his efforts in this way, "You know how I lived the whole time I was with you. . . . I have not hesitated to preach anything that would be helpful to you but have taught you publicly and from house to house." (Acts 20:18–20).

Paul's activities suggest two elements around which everything else revolved. He was *with* people and he *taught* them. Those were his primary tasks— *befriending* others and *imparting* the truth. This was the essence and genius of his ministry, the blend and balance of what he called "serving the Lord."

Paul was with others, befriending, socializing, getting to know them, entering into their lives. He reminds me of Jesus ("God *with* us"), who spent a seemingly inordinate amount of time eating, fishing, strolling by the sea, chatting, going to parties, being neighborly. You would think both Paul and Jesus would get on with it since there was so much left to do. But neither were wasting time. They were making friends.

Friend-making isn't easy, but it's simple: A friend is merely someone we befriend. Or, said another way, the way to make a friend is to be one. As the King James Version puts it, "A man that hath friends must show himself friendly" (Prov. 18:24). With that perspective in mind, no one would ever be lonely, because his whole world would be full of friends.

But friendships don't just happen. They're forged by spending time with others—working, playing, walking fields and streams together, sharing lunches, swapping yarns, hanging out. I can't think of a better way to influence others, and anyone can do it. *Anyone* can be a friend.

The other element in Paul's work was impartation: "I have not hesitated to preach anything that would be helpful to you but have taught you publicly and from house to house."

Friendship entails telling another what we ourselves have come to know about God—nothing more and nothing less. As God teaches us new things about Himself we must give those truths away. Like Jonathan, who went to David at Horesh and "helped him find strength in God" (1 Sam. 23:16), a real friend is one who leaves another with a word that strengthens his grip on God.

Befriending, then, is more than mere togetherness and small talk; it means sharing in one way or another what we've heard from God.

We won't always do it well; some of us are not especially articulate. But even an awkwardly spoken word is better than no word at all. Even the comment that seems inept can be a source of strength. And even if no fruit is immediately gathered, and our friend seems no closer to God, something has happened: A seed has been planted and the life in that seed will cause it to grow. As our Lord promised, "My word . . . will not return to me empty, but will accomplish what I desire and achieve the purpose for which I sent it" (Isa. 55:11).

Befriending and imparting. It takes hard work to maintain that balance. Some of us tend to be reflective, engaging in books and other quiet activities; others of us are more active, preferring to be with people. We're naturally inclined toward one mode or the other. But God can curb and discipline our natural tendencies. He wants symmetry for us with all His heart, and, therefore, if we ask Him to level out our lives, He will.

Such simplicity! It seems too simple to be true. But the fundamentals apply: The simplest things are often the holiest things of all.

HOUSE TO HOUSE

Warm-up: Acts 20:17–21

*I have not hesitated to preach any-
thing that would be helpful to you
but have taught you publicly
and from house to house (Acts 20:20).*

Paul distinguishes two ways to impart the truth: He taught "publicly and from house to house."

Some of our proclamation is public—teaching or preaching to people *en masse*. But there's more—that quiet and hidden work of individual and small group discipleship. Both impartations are necessary.

Richard Baxter, the old vicar of Kidderminster, wrote:

> For my part, I study to speak as plainly and as
> movingly as possible . . . and yet I frequently meet
> with those that have been my hearers eight or ten
> years, who know not whether Christ be God or
> man, and wonder when I tell them the history of
> his birth and life and death as if they had never
> heard it before . . . I have found by experience,
> that some persons, who have long been
> unprofitable hearers, have got more knowledge
> and remorse in half an hour's close discourse,
> than they did from ten year's public preaching. I
> know that preaching the gospel publicly is the
> most excellent means, because we speak to so

many at once. But it is usually far more effectual to speak it privately to a particular person.

(The Reformed Pastor)

Baxter's words remain relevant. Those who teach large groups can attest to the value of public proclamation—speaking to many at once—and to preaching's relative ineffectiveness for producing long-term discipleship. Many who hear the Word are untouched by what's said, and it appears that they're content to stay that way.

We too must look for a way to personalize the message and "speak it privately to a particular person."

There are those singular moments when people ask for comfort or counsel or for a further explanation of the truth, or those special times when we take long walks with our friends or meet them over coffee to talk about truth and its implications for life.

But one can't invest oneself in everyone. Such efforts have never been one person's task. It's rather "with all the saints" that we as individuals have the power to know all the dimensions of the knowledge of God (Eph. 3:18). Therefore, we must get the saints together to help each one grasp the truth and grow.

That's why I'm a firm believer in small groups. Small groups make truth more meaningful as Christians hear other Christians wrestling with the meaning of the Word and its implications for life. (Our groups at Cole Community Church study the same text that I teach on Sunday, which means that our people come prepared to question the text—and me!)

Small groups provide opportunities to question and search the Scriptures in a friendly, informal setting. It's okay to ask dumb questions in such a setting—to be obtuse, out of bounds, off the wall. Even "wrong" questions, when taken seriously, lead to wisdom.

Small groups give young believers an opportunity to exercise and enlarge their inner lives by rubbing shoulders with older Christians who have known Christ longer and know Him better. By laying their lives alongside the more mature they're encouraged to keep on maturing.

Small groups also provide opportunities to exercise and enlarge one's spiritual gifts. They provide protection and encouragement to neophytes taking their first steps in ministry.

Small groups provide accountability. We all need help in guarding our souls. We live in a world of illusions and lies. We're inclined to compromise with sin and its deceits, not knowing that our hearts are getting harder every day. We need someone outside of ourselves, unconvinced by our reasons for sin, who will patiently and pleasantly labor to bring us to our senses.

Small groups link sharing and caring. They're shelters of sympathy and concern. Paul encourages us to fulfill the law of love by carrying "each other's burdens" (Gal. 6:2), but large groups make this almost impossible to accomplish. We keep our weakness to ourselves in impersonal environments, but kinship groups encourage us to expose ourselves. Once others know of our burdens and share them, they're more easily borne. Feeble arms and knees are strengthened (Heb. 12:12); needs are met directly and immediately through prayer, comfort, counsel, and investment of time, work, and money.

Small groups make for loving discipline. When someone persists in sin and resists correction it's far better for two or three who know the person *well* to go and plead for repentance (Matt. 18:15–17). And then if it becomes necessary to "tell it to the church," the announcement can be made to those in the nurturing group, who make it their business to reinforce the original appeal with repeated loving contact and correction. It's more difficult to resist truth when it's delivered with deep affection by one's close friends.

I agree with George MacDonald that the "whole gathered mass is nothing but a heap of sand except in proportion to what is awakened in the hearts of individuals." If individuals don't know God, no gathering of people brings anyone nearer to the throne. God saves us and changes us one by one. The main thing is the individual person.

HUMILITY

Warm-up: Luke 14:8–11

You know how I lived the whole time I was with you. . . . I served the Lord with great humility . . . (Acts 20:18–19).

Pride inhibits friend-making. As the wise man said, "Pride only breeds quarrels" (Prov. 13:10). It separates us from God and from one another.

Pride is a terrible trait, manifesting itself in our passion for the "best seats"—insisting on recognition, wanting to be noticed, longing for prominence, smarting when we're not consulted or advised, dominating social situations. It displays itself when we resist authority or become angry and defensive when crossed or challenged; when we harbor grudges, nurse grievances, or wallow in self-pity. It's the drive behind our penchant for associating with the rich and famous rather than the little people who make up most of our world.

Humility means being led downward. It means being content when others are elevated above us and letting others advance even at our own expense. It means being glad when someone else is preferred. It means accepting every humiliation and looking upon every person who demeans us as a means of grace to humble us. God accepts such humbling as the proof that our whole heart desires it.

Charles de Foucauld's words from long ago seem singularly appropriate:

> Never think that in lowering yourself you have less power for good. On the contrary, in thus humbling yourself you are imitating and using the same means that I (Jesus) used. You are walking in my way and therefore in the truth, and you are in the right state to receive life and impart it to others.
>
> The best means for this is *my* way. I came down to the level of men by my Incarnation, and to that of sinners by my Circumcision and Baptism. Be lowly, lowly, lowly, humble, humble. Let those that are in high places put themselves last in a spirit of lowliness and service, love for men, humility, taking the lowest place so long as the divine will does not call you to another, for in that case you must obey. Obedience first of all—conformity to the will of God.
>
> If you are placed high, then keep yourself in humility of soul as though you were last; occupy your high position as though you were there only to serve others and to lead them to salvation.
>
> (Meditations of a Hermit)

The beginning place for all of us, then, is to learn humility from Jesus: He was "meek and humble in heart," not the least bit concerned about protecting His dignity or position. By coming to Him and asking for His help we'll become more like Him, and we'll find that rest of which He speaks—rest from all the ambitious striving that makes us so weary and ill at ease (cf. Matt. 11:29).

O Jesus! Meek and humble of heart, hear me.

From the desire of being esteemed,
From the desire of being loved,
From the desire of being extolled,
From the desire of being honored,
From the desire of being praised,
From the desire of being preferred to others,
From the desire of being consulted,
From the desire of being approved,
From the fear of being humiliated,
From the fear of being despised,
From the fear of suffering rebukes,
From the fear of being falsely accused,
From the fear of being forgotten,
From the fear of being ridiculed,
From the fear of being wronged,
From the fear of being suspected,

Deliver me Jesus.

That others may be loved more than I,
That others may be esteemed more than I,
That, in the opinion of the world,
    others may increase and I may decrease,
That others may be chosen and I set aside,
That others may be praised and I unnoticed,
That others may be preferred before me in
    everything,
That others become holier than I,
    provided that I may become as holy as I should,

Jesus, grant me the grace to desire it.

(*A Litany of Humility*)

COMPASSION

Warm-up: Lamentations 2:1–12

*I served the Lord with great humility
and with tears . . . (Acts 20:19).*

I'll never forget a funeral I conducted for a small child. As we waited for the family to gather, a little boy walked up to the tiny casket and gazed in. He was obviously distressed and I wanted to comfort him. "Your little sister is with Jesus," I said. Good theology. Bad timing.

He burst into tears. "I don't want her to be with Jesus," he sobbed, "I want her here with me so we can play!" I put my arm around him and we both cried.

Sometimes tears are the only thing we can do for another, the only thing we *should* do. As George MacDonald discovered, "Tears are often the only cure for weeping."

Christians aren't Stoics, striving to be pure mind without passion. Stoicism is a dehumanizing, pagan ethic; there's nothing Christian about it. It confuses discipline with suppression, reduces self-control to the repression of all emotion, and curbs all feelings in their outward expression.

Jesus' example instructs us otherwise. There was no embarrassment in His grief. When confronted with suffering, "Jesus wept" (John 11:35).

Talking is what I usually do. It's what I'm paid to do. But sometimes there are simply no words to say. I sit in silence and wait. But when words are most empty, tears are most apt. Our compassion can relieve those who suffer from the worst misery of all—the feeling of being alone in their misery. Much can be said without anything being spoken.

That kind of compassion can't be generated but it can grow on us. Being around people helps. We can't be with them very long without becoming aware of their longings and hurts. Our kinship links us to their sorrows.

Compassion also grows out of our own failure and sin. Unjudged sin can harden us and separate us from others, but sin acknowledged and repented of sensitizes us to others' frailty and draws us closer to them. Common sin is our common ground; publicans and sinners become our kind of people.

Compassion likewise grows through our own suffering. Paul reminds us that God is the source of mercy and comfort, who comforts us in all our afflictions so we can comfort others. "If we are distressed," he writes, "it is for your comfort and salvation" (2 Cor. 1:6). Personal pain is a prerequisite for consoling others. As A. W. Tozer said, "It's doubtful that God can use any man greatly until he's been hurt deeply."

We're hurt in many ways—through rejection, failure, reversal, and wrongs. We all have our own particular sorrows. Our wounds are not always scratches; sometimes they're deep and ugly and near-mortal. But God cares and cures. When earthly comforts fail us He gives "eternal encouragement" (2 Thess. 2:16). Pain moves us closer to our Father and we gain His perspective on our broken dreams; we get His comfort; "by his wounds we are healed" (Isa. 53:5).

But we get more than salve for our own wounds: We are healed so we can heal. We're made more human and humane, more kind and empathetic. We understand and people are helped by our understanding. Thus, by our wounds others are healed.

And finally, compassion comes from worship and prayer. Compassion is ultimately a gift from God. There are more seminars than ever before that aim to make us sensitive to others, but true compassion can never be the product of systematic study or effort. It is the fruit of intimacy with the God who cares for us (1 Peter 5:7).

His caring begets caring for others. His compassion rubs off on us; His love becomes ours. Our love by Love grows mighty in His love.

ADVERSITY

Warm-up: Mark 10:17–31

> *Peter said to him, "We have left*
> *everything to follow you!"*
> *"I tell you the truth," Jesus replied,*
> *"no one who has left home or brothers*
> *or sisters or mother or father or*
> *children or fields for me and the gospel*
> *will fail to receive a hundred times as*
> *much in this present age (homes,*
> *brothers, sisters, mothers, children*
> *and fields—and with them,*
> *persecutions) . . ." (Mark 10:28–30).*

Ehrman's commentary on Murphy's Law states that: (1) Things will get worse before they get better, and (2) Who says things will get better?

We believe things will get better—that God will go soft on those of us who have "left everything" to follow him, that life will get easier as we go along and we get better at what we do.

For some it is an article of faith, but God doesn't affirm that creed. He never said He would save us from the hard times; He only promised to safeguard our souls.

Christians suffer. Crosses, arenas, and scaffolds have often been the earthly reward for a job well done, and in our own more sheltered lives painful, mortifying, and expensive things keep happening to us. "Sorrow upon sorrow" is the lonely, invisible burden of every worker, and sometimes the hardest tests are further along.

Suffering happens because there are things to be done in our character that can only be accomplished through strenuous effort. Without pain we could never make the most of our ministries. The heartache He permits yields fruit: "He who goes out weeping, carrying seed to sow, will return with songs of joy, carrying sheaves with him" (Ps. 126:6).

We're inclined to fix on the ordeal, but God chooses to look forward and anticipate its effect. By disappointment, grief, tears, and even by our sin, God deals with our unworthiness in His mysterious love, breaking it down and refining it, making us wiser, sweeter, more willing to let go of what we want, more sensitive, less talkative. Suffering softens our face.

Life is sometimes tragic: Everyone suffers. What do we know of others' bitter tears unless we've shed our own? How can we speak of God's "eternal encouragement" unless we ourselves have first been comforted by God? He is indeed the "Father of compassion and the God of all comfort, who comforts us in all our troubles, so that we can comfort those in any trouble with the comfort we ourselves have received from God" (2 Cor. 1:3). Our suffering isn't meant just for us; it's also for others.

God doesn't send the hurts but He sees them coming. He could protect us but He knows that the pain will drive us to Him. Suffering kills us—shatters the illusion that we're alive apart from God—and pushes us closer to Him. And once we're near Him and begin to undergo His healing, we can bring others to Him for His help. As the Scripture says, "We . . . are always being given over to death for Jesus' sake, so that his life may be revealed in our mortal body. So then, death is at work in us, but life is at work in you" (2 Cor. 4:11–12).

"Tribulacion is medicinable," Thomas More wrote from his prison cell in London Tower, "if taken downe." Tribulation does its part, but we have our own part to play: Ours is to submit to the process and the work that must be done. There's no other way to bring life out of death.

Even Jesus was matured in His ministry through pain: "In bringing many sons into glory, it was fitting that God . . . should make the author of their salvation perfect through suffering" (Heb. 2:10). Our Lord learned what it meant to submit to suffering in this world. He was qualified for His work by agony and tears. His investment in ministry meant hard wood and nails for Him. It was "fitting" for God to mature His Son in this way; it is fitting for God to so mature us.

To resist the pain, then, is to miss the purpose of it; we must not feel sorry for ourselves. Self-pity is deadly and demonic. It's the Evil One's way of stalling us into introspection and inertia. There is no place for giving up. The warfare is much bigger than our personal humiliations. To feel sorry for oneself is totally inappropriate.

Suffering isn't fatal. Our eternal destiny isn't riding on our circumstances or on what people do or say. Our security is based upon our Lord's acceptance and His word. As He promised, with such fine irony, even though "they will put some of you to death . . . not a hair of your head will perish" (Luke 21:16, 18). The only fatal act is to give up.

Someday our Lord will return to gather us in and heal us once-and-for-all of our terrible wounds. In the meantime, we mustn't waste our pain. Suffering promotes counsel we could not otherwise give and messages that we could not otherwise deliver.

Life is not as idle ore
   But iron dug from central gloom,
And heated hot with burning fears,
   And dipt in baths of hissing tears,
And battered by the shocks of doom
   To shape and use.

GUARDING OURSELVES

Warm-up: 1 Timothy 4:6–16

*Keep watch over yourselves and all
the flock of which the Holy Spirit
has made you overseers (Acts 20:28).*

We can expect attacks on the sheep—savage wolves
from without and wolves in sheep's clothing from
within. So, as Paul warns, "Keep watch over yourselves
and all the flock. . . ." Guarding others begins with
guarding ourselves. On this preoccupation everything
depends. As the wise man said, "Above all else, guard
your heart" (Prov. 4:23).

Søren Kierkegaard wrote in his journal that "would-
be theologians . . . must be on their guard lest by
beginning too soon to preach they rather chatter
themselves into Christianity than live themselves into
it and find themselves at home there."

What he writes about would-be theologians remains
an occupational hazard for all of us: How easy it is to
chatter on about a God we do not know and traffic in
unlived truth. We should heed James' warning about
speakers being more likely to be hypocrites than anyone
else (James 3:1–12).

Paul said to Timothy, "Watch your life and doctrine
closely. Persevere in them, because if you do, you will
save both yourself and your hearers" (1 Tim. 4:16). It's
vital to stay in touch with God. The alternative is to do

damage to ourselves and to those we want to help. If our personal lives are disordered, others' lives will also be in disarray. We must take care of ourselves first. By doing so we take the first step in saving others.

Life drains us. There is the ministry itself—working with others, planning activities, studying, thinking, preparing messages. There's the monotony of doing the same things day after day—dozens of tedious endeavors. And then there is our own everyday job of fighting temptation, suppressing our passions, working with God to correct our faults. Our work gets to be wearisome and our energy ebbs away. We need perpetual renewing of our original impulse, drive, and desires; like a spring-driven clock we need to be wound up again.

And so we need our solitude, not mere privacy and time alone, but time alone with God, a regular, specific time and place to read His Word, to pray, to worship, a beginning place from which we can practice God's presence through the day. "Without solitude," Henri Nouwen wrote, "it is virtually impossible to live a spiritual life." Solitude begins with a time and place for God, and Him alone. If we really believe not only that God exists but that He is actively present in our lives—healing, teaching, and guiding—we need to set aside a time and space to give Him our undivided attention. Jesus said, "Go into your room, close the door, and pray to your Father, who is unseen" (Matt. 6:6).

Oswald Chambers said, "The only way to survive in ministry is to steadfastly refuse to be interested in ministry and to be interested only in Jesus Christ." Without that preoccupation, we have nothing to say and no reason to serve.

But how do I manage it? Something or someone always opposes me; my best resolutions go awry; I find it hard to get to that secret place and shut the door.

When I was a much younger man, I met with an earnest friend who invited me to join him in developing a "consistent quiet time," as he put it. I knew that prayer and worship was my primary task, and I wanted more than anything else to learn how it was done, but his plan never worked for me. I couldn't get the hang of it.

I'd stay with his scheme for a week or two, rising very early each morning to agonize my way through a regimen of prayer. It was a discipline I imposed on myself—somewhat like devoting oneself to doing fifty push-ups every day. I knew the program would be good for me, but I hated the drill and in time I gave it up, believing that I wasn't one of those destined for meditation and prayer.

It wasn't until much later that I stumbled across something that changed my mind—something David said: "My heart says of you, 'Seek his face!' Your face, LORD, I will seek" (Ps. 27:8). I realized for the first time that the first move was God's. He was taking the initiative to meet with me! Those deep longings to be alone with him were not mine at all, but His. My desire to meet with God was His voice calling out to me, saying, "Seek my face."

And then I recalled what Jesus said to the woman at the well—almost a throw-away line—about the Father *seeking* us to worship Him (John 4:23). It's that idea of God wanting me, seeking me, *missing* me that renewed my soul.

And so He calls to me—His depths to mine. Deep

within God and within me, it seems, there is a place for just the two of us, and without that fellowship we both ache in loneliness and emptiness.

And so I have come to believe that worship is not a matter of my trying to get God's attention, but of my listening for the call of God. I am not the seeker, He initiates my love. Worship is my response to Him as He reaches out to me, speaking to me. And, as a friend once said, "It's up to me to be polite enough to pay attention."

G. K. Chesterton said that the whole Bible is about the "loneliness" of God. That's a new way of thinking about Him—to believe that what He always wanted was my love; that though He knows every urge of my mean little heart, He still likes me and wants to be my friend (cf. John 15:15); that in some mysterious way, He not only wants me but actually *needs* me and calls me to seek His face. The idea that my longing is actually His voice calling—that idea alone—has changed the way I look at my quiet moments with God. They are now neither duty nor discipline, but rather an answer to one who wants to know me and to be known.

The *Psalter Hymnal* includes this wise anthem:

I sought the Lord, and afterward I knew
    He moved my soul to seek Him, seeking me;
It was not I that found, O Savior true,
    No, I was found of Thee.

Thou didst reach forth Thy hand and mine enfold;
    I walked and sank not on the storm-vexed sea,
'Twas not so much that I on Thee took hold,
    As Thou, dear Lord, on me.

A Burden Shared

I find, I walk, I love, but O the whole
    Of love is but my answer, Lord, to Thee:
For Thou wert long beforehand with my soul,
    Always Thou lovest me.

AUTHORITY

Warm-up: Luke 22:24–30

*The greatest among you should be
like the youngest, and the one who
rules like the one who serves
(Luke 22:26).*

I recall a character in Shakespeare's *King Henry IV* who claimed that he could "call up spirits from the vasty deep." "Why, so can I, or so can any man" was the rejoinder. "But will they come when you do call for them?"

The question of authority is a good one to raise, particularly when someone's claim seems inflated. It's one thing to assert authority; it's another to possess it.

Unauthorized power goes directly to people's heads. According to Acton's dictum, power corrupts and absolute power corrupts absolutely. You see it all the time—ego-driven men and women, motivated by a gluttonous lust for power and money, who manipulate or bully others into submission. Unfortunately, power's seduction can also corrupt those of us who lead the church, alluring us into thinking more highly of ourselves than we ought to think, enticing us into dominating others, like the overpowering Diotrephes, of whom John said, "who loves to be *first*" (3 John 9, emphasis added).

Jesus teaches us otherwise: He said to His disciples

(when a dispute arose among them concerning who was the greatest), "The kings of the Gentiles lord it over them; and those who exercise authority over them call themselves Benefactors. But you are not to be like that. Instead, the greatest among you should be like the youngest, and the one who rules like the one who serves. For who is greater, the one who is at the table or the one who serves? Is it not the one who is at the table? But I am among you as one who serves" (Luke 22:25–26).

The model of leadership in Jesus day was the corporate model—bossing, patronizing, commanding, controlling, and expecting gratitude for the slightest acts of kindness.

Jesus, on the other hand, was a secondary, self-sacrificing figure, who demanded nothing of others and expected nothing for Himself. His manner was lowly; His symbol was a slave down on his knees with a towel and a washbasin (John 13:2–5).

Though he "had all authority in heaven and earth," He never pulled rank nor insisted on His way. His leadership was not lordship but servanthood. He preferred others and deferred to their needs. He led by service, gentle persuasion, and love. His model of authority and leadership is not a mere softening of secular leadership, but a radically different disposition. His call to leadership is a call to humility, self-death, and servitude to others.

It would never do for us to contradict our Lord. We are not greater than our master (John 13:16). Our leadership must be like His. The measure of our authority is not how many are "under our ministries," as we like to say, but rather how many we are under.

The best thing for us, then, is to get off our pedestals

and power trips and, like Jesus, get down on our knees. Leadership means just that—being lower than all, washing their feet, being their "servants for Jesus' sake" (2 Cor. 4:5).

It means preferring others, furthering their causes, seeking their good, encouraging their growth, bearing their evil (as long as it does not corrupt others), being gentle and humble—doing for others what God Himself has done for us.

It means leading by persuasion, reason, and proclamation of the Word of God, rather than by personal mandate and ultimatum. We cannot dictate or demand. We can only declare.

And then, when all is said and done, we should forget what we have done. We should acknowledge that, "We are unworthy servants; we have only done our duty" (Luke 17:10).

But never fear: We'll never lose out by so losing ourselves. Servitude is the basis of true significance. "The great leader is seen as a servant first, and that simple fact is the key to his greatness," as Robert K. Greenleaf said. No one in this world is taken lightly who cares for others and who lightens their load.

But, you say, despite my efforts to serve, some still do not take me seriously.

Look for another way to serve those who deprecate you, recalling that God Himself put down our resistance, not by sheer power but by servitude. If that's what He did, it's all that we can do.

That was Paul's counsel to Timothy: "Don't let anyone look down on you because you are young, but set an example for the believers in speech, in life, in love, in faith and in purity. Until I come, devote yourself to the public reading of Scripture, to preaching and to teaching. Do not neglect your gift . . ." (1 Tim. 4:12).

Timothy was a relative youngster in a culture where young men were generally disregarded. Being venerable was the thing. But Paul's words suggest that the problem is never youth nor inexperience; it's immaturity.

If we're growing in grace and faithfully using our gifts, we'll be influencing others toward God, whether we know it or not, and, after all, having the ability to influence others toward God is what legitimate authority is all about.

And what will that influence look like? At first it may not look like anything at all. Spiritual power is never apparent. It isn't a matter of charm and chutzpah, nor is it a function of vast knowledge, strength of will, or personal magnetism.

Servant authority is more implicit and imperceptible. It's not obvious to others or to ourselves. (Self-conscious influence is readily lost.) It's an unaffected and quiet persuasion that pervades another's thoughts and gently goads them toward God's will and His righteousness.

It's the authority of the Servant of the Lord: "Here is my servant, whom I uphold, my chosen one in whom I delight; I will put my Spirit on him and he will bring justice to the nations. He will not shout or cry out, or raise his voice in the streets. A bruised reed he will not break, and a smoldering wick he will not snuff out. . . . He will not falter or be discouraged til he establishes justice on earth. In his law the islands will put their hope" (Isa. 42:1–4).

THE COURSE

Warm-up: Acts 20:22–24

I consider my life worth nothing to me, if only I may finish the race [course] and complete the task the Lord Jesus has given me . . . (Acts 20:24).

I have fought the good fight, I have finished the race [course] (2 Tim. 4:7).

I have a hunter-friend who gets himself lost in the backcountry every year. But, as he explains, he's never really lost. Though he takes the queerest route through the woods, he's always headed for home.

Paul had the same optimism. Often lost, he was always going in the right direction.

Two elements characterized his outlook: There was a *course* to be run and a *task* to be done. He knew his task—to testify solemnly of the grace of God—but as to his course he hadn't a clue. He had no fixed and final five-year plan.

And so, on one occasion, off he went to Jerusalem counting on God to chart his course and starting himself on a journey no one ever could have planned.

His witness in that city touched off a riot. He was arrested and sent to Caesaria, where he was jailed for two years waiting for the court's decision then shipped to the city of Rome, where he was placed under house arrest for two more years. (The book of Acts ends at this point.) While confined in Rome, Paul was chained to members of Caesar's Praetorian Guard, the elite young men of the empire, most of whom, after serving in the military, became the mind-movers and king-makers of the Roman Empire. They were shackled to the apostle in four hour shifts, looking over his shoulder as he penned his letters, listening as he debated and defended his gospel with those who came to visit. They heard him "testifying to the gospel of God's grace."

Paul's pregnant greeting from "those who belong to Caesar's household" to his friends in Philippi (Phil. 4:22) suggests that some of these young soldiers, members of Caesar's household, were becoming members of the household of faith and taking the gospel to the nerve-center of the Roman Empire. Who could have premeditated or planned that course?

We too have a task to undertake and a course to follow. We know the task—to "testify to the gospel of God's grace." We're on our way to the next turn in our course, "not knowing what will happen to [us] there."

But we don't have to wonder what God will do with us. He knows the unknown and will go before us and lead us where others have never gone before and where we've never thought that we could go. Following Him takes us beyond anything we could ever ask or imagine (Eph. 3:20).

That's why we Christians sometimes do the oddest and most unorthodox things. Certainly, we have orthodox plans and prepare in ordinary ways and harbor our dreams like others. But we must hold our schemes and schedules loosely, giving God the right to chart and change our course.

This means that we will not know what will happen to us next. We'll be out of control, living with uncertainty, giving up the security of our own plans, existing in a world where God's will is the only sure thing.

But God's will means that every one of our moments is managed by Him. Our course is His business, not ours. Our task is to "testify to the gospel of God's grace." His is to get us to the right person at the right place at the right time.

> Perhaps by a friend far distant,
>   Perhaps by a stranger near,
> Perhaps by a spoken message,
>   Perhaps by the printed word.
>
> Perhaps by a single angel,
>   Perhaps by a mighty host,
> Perhaps by the chain that frets me,
>   Or the walls that shut me in.
>
> Perhaps by a door wide open,
>   Perhaps by a door fast barred,
> Perhaps by a joy withholden,
>   Perhaps by a gladness given.
>
> Perhaps by a plan accomplished,
>   Perhaps when He stays my hand,
> Perhaps by a word in season,
>   Perhaps by a silent prayer.
>   —Annie Johnson Flint

Keeping that perspective on our course keeps us from comparing ourselves with others. When we wonder why another is given a different course to follow, we hear Him say, "What is that to you? You must follow me" (John 21:22). Imitation—doing what God wants *others* to do—keeps us from doing what God wants *us* to do. But if we keep to His course He will make us an original—an instrument incomparably useful and uniquely crafted to do the Master's work (2 Tim. 2:21).

Keeping that perspective also makes us more creative than we ever thought possible. We don't go by the book. We can't be pinned down, predicted, programmed, controlled, or classified. We don't initiate anything, yet innovation is inevitable when we follow Him.

And finally, keeping that perspective keeps us on course. If we trust Him with all of our heart and acknowledge Him in all our ways, we're assured that He'll direct our paths (Prov. 3:6). Those who do not want God's will, miss it, but the one who is "firmly settled upon this, 'Whatever God tells me, God helping me I am going to do,' will not be left in doubt as to what God does wish him to do" (Alexander McLaren).

And in the end, our course will be clear. Looking back, Paul could see all the pieces and puzzles of his life as part of a coherent whole and declare, "I have finished the [course] . . ." (2 Tim. 4:7).

The course, which must be lived in prospect, can only be understood in retrospect. Thus, God sanctifies our memories—as we look back over the path of past obedience we see what He has been doing with us all along.

THE PURPOSE

Warm-up: Colossians 1:24–29

Now I commit you to God and to the word of his grace, which can build you up and give you an inheritance among all those who are sanctified (Acts 20:32).

"What in the world are you doing to these people?" the plaque on the old pulpit read. I couldn't get my eyes or my mind off of it. It's one of the best questions I've ever been asked!

What was I doing to the people in my care? Did I have any objective for them? Was there some ultimate purpose, or was I simply being carried along, doing what busy workers do—presiding over solemn traditions, herding sacred cows, doing the usual? What in the world was I doing to these people? I wasn't sure I knew.

I'm happy to say that Paul had better aim. He had one objective—to leave men and women with God and with the word of His grace. With that legacy his people could come into their own.

The goal of all ministry is to enable men and women to be grown-up disciples who are independently dependent on Christ and His Word. That's the purpose for which every other purpose exists. As Paul says elsewhere, "We proclaim him, admonishing and teaching everyone with all wisdom, *so that we may present everyone* [*mature*] *in Christ*. To this end I labor, struggling with all his energy, which so powerfully works in me" (Col. 1:28–29, emphasis added).

Evangelizing, discipling, counseling, advising, organizing, encouraging, and socializing exist for one purpose and one purpose alone: To encourage women and men to become grown-up disciples of Christ. There's simply no other reason for doing what we do.

Maturity, of course, is a growing thing: No one ever arrives in this life. But maturity, to the extent that any of us is mature, is a matter of moving toward the fullness of Christ, the acquisition of all that He has for us. "All of us who are mature," as Paul explains, "should take such a view of things" (Phil. 3:15).

And so this question must be put to every endeavor: Is this activity in which I'm so busily engaged helping others mature? If not, it's not worth doing much longer.

Some tasks are plainly for maturing. Other activities are less obvious, and their fruit may be deferred. Some of our efforts to befriend others, for example, may seem unproductive in the beginning. But our aim for every endeavor should be to see others growing toward God, and if our programs and projects do not contribute to that end we have no good reason to perpetuate them, no matter how venerable or venerated they may be.

Although we must be sensitive in doing away with extraneous endeavors, we should gently move toward doing only those things that matter, the activities that lead to growth.

And so, I keep asking myself, "What in the world are you doing to these people? What are you leaving behind?"

I trust that our legacy, like Paul's, is maturity, and that after our departure it's said of us that we too left others stubbornly clinging to God and to His Word. May our epitaph show that we faithfully proclaimed Christ, "admonishing and teaching everyone . . . so that we may present *everyone* [mature] in Christ.

"To this end [we] labor, struggling with all his energy, which so powerfully works in [us]" (Col. 1:28–29, emphasis added).

THE MESSENGER

Warm-up: Malachi 2:1–9

The lips of a priest ought to preserve knowledge . . .
(Mal. 2:7).

Malachi was a fifth century B.C. prophet who came to indict the clergy: "The lips of a priest ought to preserve knowledge," he said, "and from his mouth men should seek instruction—because he is the messenger of the LORD Almighty. But you have turned from the way and by your teaching have caused many to stumble. . . . So I have caused you to be despised and humiliated before all the people" (2:7–9).

Malachi's complaint is valid. If the messenger doesn't take God's word seriously, no one will take him seriously—an observation analogous to Jesus' dictum about salt losing its saltiness, being thrown out and trampled under foot (Matt. 5:13). When we have nothing from God to say, we're good for nothing.

It's happening these days. We read many books but neglect the Book. We have no authority, and our people know it. We have lost the right to be heard.

We're allowed to hang around, of course; tradition demands it. We show up at official functions and render benedictions and such, but no one expects us to do anything more. Anything more and we'd only be in the way.

Henri Nouwen tells of an incident that occurred when he was chaplain of the Cunnard Line ocean vessel during a violent storm. Nouwen joined the captain on the bridge and waited for an opportunity to speak while the captain anxiously paced the deck.

At one point Nouwen attempted to walk with the officer, but the ship lurched and he fell into the man, nearly knocking him down. "Chaplain," the captain shouted, "get out of my way! If I want anything from you I'll let you know!"

Nouwen saw a parable: When substantive issues were at stake, as far as the captain was concerned, the messenger had nothing important to say.

Some of us may not be hearing what God is saying, and, thus, we no longer have anything to say. And since we've had nothing to say for such a long time, no one expects us to breech the long silence. We have no word for our world.

On the other hand consider the servant of the Lord: "The Sovereign LORD has given me an instructed tongue, to know the word that sustains the weary. He wakens me morning by morning, wakens my ear to listen like one being taught" (Isa. 50:4).

The servant of the Lord had something important to say because he had apprenticed himself to his Lord. He didn't speak from himself; *he* didn't have anything to say. But every morning he was awakened and enlightened by God's word and thus had a word for the weary.

If we have nothing to say to people we should wake up and act. By hiding ourselves in God, plumbing His depths, pondering His instruction, and praying for His understanding, we can then rise and speak wisdom out of that secret place.

Let us then enter our studies, and remember our preparation for our public work. . . . What has become of all those hours which we professed to spend in prayer before God, with the Bible in our hands, and our ministry in our hearts? How much time have we frittered away in vain reading; in the gratification of curiosity; in reading the last new book on divinity; in examining the last new criticism; in amusing our minds with the last review, the last piece of history, the last philosophical dissertation? I speak not against any department of sound and manly knowledge; in its place, and to certain ministers at certain times, each is indispensable. But have we kept things in their places? Have they not superseded other more immediate duties? And in the preparing of our sermons, alas, how cold, how formal have we often been. Prayer has been the last thing we have thought of, instead of being the first. We have made dissertations, not sermons; we have consulted commentators, not our Bibles; we have been led by science, not by the heart; and therefore have our discourse in public, and our instructions in private, been so tame, so lifeless, so uninteresting to the mass of the hearers, so little savoring of Christ, so little like the inspired example of St. Paul.
—Daniel Wilson, Bishop of Calcutta, 1829

APPEARANCES

Warm-up: Matthew 23:1–12

*Everything they do is done
for men to see (Matt. 23:5).*

The media caricatures Christian workers as bigots, buffoons, wimps, and bores. Their bias bothers me, but if that's their impression of us, we may have only ourselves to blame.

We often take ourselves too seriously, preoccupied with maintaining the dignity (if not the pomposity) of the office, trying to keep up appearances, striving to look tremendously important.

There are those odd mannerisms we affect—the stained-glass tones or nasal twangs with which we speak, our unctuous formality, our nervous affability—a dozen distracting idiosyncrasies.

More serious is our inclination to pontificate, to move into the center of every circle, to insist upon recognition. There is our yen for special honor, the need to be noticed, needed, included, consulted, and briefed, that prickly defensiveness that bleeds at a touch or reacts to slights with tooth and claw.

There is our aloofness and stand-offish piety that borders on transcendence, which may give the impression that we're above it all.

If the media portrayal is accurate and not a parody,

then it's all very sad: Our pretensions make us seem meddlesome and irrelevant. We alienate the world and we separate ourselves from those we're called to serve.

Our posturing may come from our infatuation with the *role* of a worker. We're concerned with the look of things rather than the things themselves. Shepherding, on the other hand, is essentially not thinking about being a shepherd at all, but rather keeping our eyes on the Chief Shepherd and seeing ourselves and others in relationship to Him. He provides the image for our reflection.

He was quiet; He did not "shout or cry out, or raise his voice in the streets" (Isa. 42:2). (Preaching was not a profession then.) He was very gentle with the weak and wayward, He blew on the smoking flaxes and tied up the broken reeds. His manner was lowly; His methods unsophisticated and unpretentious; He hated formality. He was absorbed with little people, always approachable.

He was so much like the common folk—one of the brothers (Heb. 2:11). He was, in fact, a layman (not a Levite) and so much unlike the clergy of His day, of whom He said, "Everything they do is done for men to see: They make their phylacteries wide and the tassels on their garments long; they love the place of honor at banquets and the most important seats in the synagogues; they love to be greeted in the marketplaces and to have men call them 'Rabbi' [Reverend?]. But you are not to be called 'Rabbi' for you have only one Master and *you are all brothers*" (Matt. 23:8, emphasis added).

We must take His words to heart. We're all just brothers. Nothing less and nothing more.

Now that we have been reborn, as I have said, in the likeness of our Lord, and have indeed been adopted by God as his children, let us put on the complete image of our creator, so as to be wholly like him, not in the glory that he alone possesses, but in innocence, simplicity, gentleness, patience, humility, mercy, harmony, those qualities in which he chose to become, and to be with us.

—Peter Chrysologos

CRITICISM

Warm-up: 2 Samuel 16:1–14

Leave him alone; let him curse,
for the LORD has told him to. It may be
that the LORD will see my distress and
repay me with good for the cursing I am
receiving today (2 Sam. 16:11–12).

I often ponder the plight of my friends who are out of the ministry not because of God's call but because of people's criticism. Disapproval, vented from their congregations, fell on them like acid rain, eroding their will to serve. I can understand why they gave up. I grieve for them.

God's workers may have it worse than others. We're like lightning rods drawing criticism. There are reasons for it, and sometimes we're to blame. Despite good hearts and good intentions we may be going about the task in the wrong way. In such cases we need to listen to what people have to say even if it hurts.

Spurgeon said, "Get a friend to tell you your faults, or better still, welcome an enemy who will watch you keenly and sting you savagely. What a blessing such an irritating critic will be to a wise man. What an intolerable nuisance to a fool."

But sometimes the criticism is unfair: We're set upon by men and women who have unrealistic expectations of us, who do not realize that we too are failures in need of forgiveness. Or perhaps they have a personal axe to grind: they want to deflect blame away from themselves. Or they may represent a power block in the church and resent our leadership. They criticize us because it makes them feel better about themselves.

Criticism always comes when we least need it. The assaults rarely come when we're up and on top of things. They come along with some other failure or fiasco, on the heels of another blow. It's usually when we're down and out that some critic gets going.

Furthermore, criticism seems to come when we least deserve it. We all fail at times, but it's usually when we're innocent of any wrong-doing that we're subjected to relentless and unjust attack. We don't then quite deserve the curses.

And then, criticism comes from people who are least qualified to give it. Many of the hard shots come from people who simply don't know what they're talking about, or who themselves are so morally unqualified they have no right to criticize. Some are self-serving; some have no heart for God. Yet often these are the people from whom we receive the hardest words.

And finally, criticism frequently comes in a form that is least helpful to us. It's hard enough to hear criticism when it comes in love, but no one likes to hear it when it's hard and harsh. It would be good if all critics were constructive, but that's not always the case. They aren't always redemptive; sometimes they just like to throw stones.

Since some critics, either through ignorance or willfullness, will not handle the matter appropriately, how should we respond?

First, we should acknowledge God's hand in the matter. "The LORD has told him," David said of Shimei's brutal attack upon him (2 Sam.16:11). He understood that sometimes it's God's will to bruise His own. We need to hear the criticism, even if it comes in the wrong way, for it's sometimes God's finger, pointing out some wrong in us or something wrong with our ways. "Consider the source," we say, but actually we shouldn't consider the source. We should rather, consider the criticism. There may be something to it, particularly if we hear it from more than one. As an old Yiddish proverb says, "If one man calls you an ass, pay him no mind. If two men call you an ass, go get a saddle."

But even if the criticism is untrue and unjust it will still do us good because successful living entails learning how to suffer injustice successfully. Our Lord was wrongly nailed to a cross. You can count on it that someday someone will unjustly nail you to the wall!

Being crucified is a painful process but it always results in a new quality of life. We learn meekness: We're taught to absorb abuse without retaliation, to accept criticism without defensiveness, to give a soft answer in response to another's wrath.

Second, we should not try to defend ourselves. We can take every criticism to our Advocate and ask Him to vindicate us. "He stands at the right hand of the needy one, to save his life from those who condemn him" (Ps. 109:31). We can get in God's way when we try to protect ourselves from harm. We can explain ourselves to some extent, but we cannot justify ourselves, nor should we try. With Augustine we should pray again and again, "Heal me of this lust of mine of always vindicating myself."

"Let them talk," said Alexander Whyte. "Let them write; let them correct you; let them traduce you; let them judge and condemn you; let them slay you. . . . Oh the detestable passions that corrections and contradictions kindle up to fury in the proud heart of man! Eschew controversy as you would eschew the entrance into hell itself. Let them have their way."

One thing more about critics. Remember our Lord's words: "Love your enemies and pray for those who persecute you, that you may be sons of your Father in heaven. He causes his sun to rise on the evil and the good, and sends rain on the righteous and the unrighteous. If you love those who love you, what reward will you get? Are not even the tax collectors doing that? And if you greet only your brothers, what are you doing more than others? Do not even pagans do that? Be perfect, therefore, as your heavenly Father is perfect" (Matt. 5:44).

We can forgive our enemies as Jesus did and refuse to withdraw from them or wrong them in any way. Think of Judas and Jesus' perfect love for him; although our Lord knew all along who would sell him out, not one of the other apostles knew (John 13:22)! Jesus never betrayed the betrayer.

We should then pray as George MacDonald prayed, "Make me into a rock which swallows up the waves of wrong in its great caverns and never throws them back to swell the commotion of the angry sea from whence they came. Ah! To annihilate wrong in this way—to say, 'It shall not be wrong against me, so utterly do I forgive it!' "

THE ONLY WAY TO GO

Warm-up: John 12:20–26

Unless a kernel of wheat falls to the ground and dies, it remains only a single seed. But if it dies, it produces many seeds (John 12:24).

One of the most striking paradoxes in Jesus' teaching is his idea of saving one's life by losing it. He said that dying is necessary. Those who lose their lives for Christ's sake reap a harvest of character and influence on others. Those who try to save their lives are left alone in the end, like the dear lonely woman whose epitaph read:

> Here lie the bones of Nancy Jones.
>> For her life held no terrors.
> She lived an old maid,
>> She died an old maid,
> No hits, no runs, no errors.

Being an old maid is not a matter of age, sex, or station in life but rather a matter of outlook. (The nicest old maid I ever met was a twenty-five-year-old male graduate student.) Some strive to protect themselves and find themselves worse off than before; others fling away their lives in service to Christ and those in need and find themselves transformed.

Jesus stated the principle more than once (cf. Luke 9:24; 17:33; John 12:25) and He said it in different ways:

"Give, and it will be given to you. A good measure, pressed down, shaken together and running over, will be poured into your lap. For with the measure you use it will be measured to you" (Luke 6:38). It must be a very important truth.

You'd think that if you went about dying, you'd die, but you don't. It's the other way around: Those who try to live are the ones who die. Those who insist on their rights, who never give in, who lavish care on themselves, who think only of their own place, who are obsessed with looking out for themselves, are almost always insecure and unhealthy.

But if we die to ourselves for Jesus' sake, our self-worth will never suffer. God grants worth to us. Those who feel most secure and most significant are those who have given themselves up for others. Jesus was right: Trying to find yourself is suicidal. The only way to find yourself is to lose yourself. Only what dies can be resurrected. Dying is the only way to go.

This principle holds up in every phase of life: We gain ground by giving it up. If we look for love we'll not find it, but if we give love away we'll be loved. If we search for a friend we'll not find one, but if we befriend another we'll have a good friend. If we're emotionally down and out and looking for a lift we may look forever, but if we look for ways to encourage others we'll be encouraged. If we think others should serve us, we've got another thing coming, but if we serve others for Christ's sake our real needs will be met. It's odd that it works this way. It's just backward to us, but that's the way it is. Jesus said so and He lived it: The Son of Man came to give His life a ransom for many. He was dying all of His life.

The principle holds true in the church as well. If we try to hang on to our members we'll lose them in the end. (They're not even ours to hold on to; they belong to God.) It's much better to give them away to serve more needy churches nearby. And if we hoard our financial resources and discourage our givers from other important interests, we'll never have enough for ourselves. But if we encourage God's people to give to meet real needs wherever they exist, we'll have enough money to meet our own.

Of course there's a balance; there are times when we shouldn't give. Sometimes giving only perpetuates selfishness in another or prevents them from learning from the hard times. We don't always give our children what they want; love may dictate refusal. But that's a different matter than self-centered accumulation.

The proverb states, "Do not withhold good from those who deserve it, when it is in your power to act. Do not say to your neighbor, 'Come back later; I'll give it tomorrow'—when you now have it with you" (Prov. 3:27–28). In other words, if you can give, and it's good to give, then give!

It seems that all of us tend to get more conservative as we get older. I see it in myself; I see it in our church. We get provincial and protective of our interests, playing with less abandon. We lose that go-for-broke mentality that's born of authentic faith. But we shouldn't fall for that sin; we mustn't be acquisitive and greedy. We must give ourselves away—our love, our friendship, our time, our money, our resources. The alternative is to be left like Absolom with a monument to oneself and a barren house. We must give. It's a matter of survival.

GOD'S FOOLS

Warm-up: 1 Corinthians 1:18–31

*Not many of you were wise by
human standards; not many were
influential; not many were of
noble birth (1 Cor. 1:26).*

I read that H. L. Mencken considered serious Christians
the "boobs of religion." Of course we are. Whoever
thought otherwise?

There are some who richly deserve that epithet—
deserve it in the fullest sense. Who can justify the
Crusades, pogroms against Jews, Apartheid, colonial-
ism, the Ku Klux Klan, the Inquisition, the Aryan
Nation, churchmen throughout church history
burning one another at the stake, and all the other
atrocious and ungodly things so-called Christians have
done *ad majorem glorium Dei*? Sometimes we do act
like fools.

But we should understand that there's another sense
in which we Christians are foolish. Even the apostle
Paul said, in this way, that we're fools: "Think of what
you were when you were called," he wrote. "Not many
of you were wise by human standards; not many were
influential; not many were of noble birth. But God
chose the foolish things of the world to shame the wise
. . ." (1 Cor. 1:26–27). It's not that he had to make-do
with us. He prefers us; he *chooses* fools.

Frederick Buechner marvels at what he calls "the folly [of God] to choose for his holy work in the world . . . former lamebrains and misfits and nit-pickers and . . . stuffed shirts and odd ducks and milquetoasts. . . ."

Oh, there are some among us who are rich and famous. But most of us are ordinary, garden-variety people, unimportant, insignificant, and unnecessary by the world's standard. Few have much clout; we're neither superstars nor super saints. Like St. Francis's "Jesters of God," we're the joke that God is playing on the world.

Paul's reference to God's absurdity is wedged purposefully into a letter in which he contrasts human wisdom with the wisdom of God. Secular scholars, he notes, impressed with their education and intellect and glorying in their credentials and degrees, take heart in what man can know and can do for himself.

God, on the other hand, is content to work with regular folks; His wisdom stresses human weakness and limitation. That's why Christians seem foolish in a world that makes so much of man.

I've spent a lot of time hanging out in the halls of scholarship. (Carolyn refers to me as her academia nut.) I've done time in several major institutions. I've learned a lot of facts and one great lesson: You can't expect to be a serious follower of Jesus and be taken seriously.

You can talk about things that are good and true and beautiful on these campuses and the atmosphere will remain warm and friendly. But refer to God as someone who is real, personal, and knowable and people will look at you as though you announced that you've recently become a member of The Flat Earth Society.

You can even learn the Bible in these classrooms and still be thought of as learned, as long as you only talk about the niceties of the text, its relationship to Hittite Covenant Law, and how the Hebrew hiphil stem applies. But let it be known that you really believe in the Incarnation, the Cross, and the Resurrection, and you'll go from being a sage to being a fool.

But not to worry: Lots of folks thought Jesus was a fool too. The distinguished scholars of His day considered themselves far more literate, knowledgeable, and enlightened than He. He was nothing more than an itinerant street preacher with no formal schooling or sheepskin; He was the village embarrassment. And so it will always be.

We mustn't be anti-intellectual; certainly scholarship has its place in Christianity. But so much of man's scholarship has so little to do with learning. It's more about being *learned*, or rather, about the *appearance* of being learned. It's often nothing more than a cover-up for intellectual pride.

There's so much affectation and humbug in the field—the elitism, the pedantry, the love of the subtle and clever put-down, even the uniform dress code—the beard, the longish hair, the briar pipe, the scruffy tweed coat, the baggy cords, the heeled-over Hush Puppies. The affectations are on the surface, but the snobbery and arrogance goes clear to the bone—in contrast to Jesus, who was "meek and humble in heart."

Scholars tend to be much too enamored with their minds. It's appealing to believe that human beings can make it on their own—that intellect and education will bring them home free (wherever home may be).

But that's a serious mistake. It's not that intellectual pride is just an unfortunate little trait and humility is an attractive little virtue. Intellectual pride is suicidal; it's what separates us from the life of God.

As Paul would say, the world through its wisdom did not, indeed, *cannot* know God (cf. 1 Cor. 1:21). "All our knowledge only brings us closer to our ignorance, and all our ignorance closer to death, but closer to death, no nearer to God" (T. S. Eliot).

No, there has to be another way, and there is: It's the way of Jesus, who told us that truly happy folks in this world are those who are poor in spirit (Matt. 5:3). These are the people who are wise enough to know that they don't have it made and can't make it, who realize that the world's wisdom will never lead them to God. These are the men and women whom God is making more alive every day because they have chosen to believe in the foolishness of the cross (1 Cor. 1:18). They know that what they cannot do for themselves, Another has done for them.

BEING SINGLEMINDED

Warm-up: 1 Corinthians 7:1–40

*Each one should retain the place in
life that the Lord assigned to
him and to which God has called
him (1 Cor. 7:17).*

The poet Robert Service once observed that "there's a race of men that don't fit in." In the world today that race would have to be represented by God's single servants.

Unmarried men are especially suspect: We're told, by people who are supposed to know these things, that they're three times more prone to nervous breakdown than married men and more disposed to crime, drugs, alcoholism, and violence. They're more irresponsible about their debts, more accident prone, more susceptible to disease. Their mortality rate is almost double that of married men and three times the rate of single women, and suicide is increasingly the way they die.

Furthermore, we're told that single men are full of sexual urgency and ego-sensitivity, and known for vain posturing and tall stories. They try too hard, which is why they are not only single but alone. Art Hoppe, columnist for the *San Francisco Chronicle*, recently quoted an older, single man who walked out of a bar by himself, put on his hat, and said quietly to himself, "My place or mine?"

All of this may lead us to believe that there's something dreadfully wrong with being unmarried. If not sinful, being spouseless is at least considered strange, and especially strange are those hardy souls who remain unmarried after they're over the hill. "So why aren't you married yet?" is the opening gambit of all match-making mothers, as though you're fundamentally weird if you're not married.

Yet, isn't it odd that we denigrate the single state, when our Lord, the only sinless, perfect man who ever lived, wasn't married? That's very odd indeed.

It's enough that Jesus was a bachelor, but we have more. We have His explicit teaching on single living. When His disciples complained that His teaching on staying married was too hot to handle and concluded that it might be better not to marry, Jesus actually agreed with them. He continued, "Not everyone can accept this word, but only those to whom it has been given. For some . . . have renounced marriage because of the kingdom of heaven. The one who can accept this should accept it" (Matthew 19:11–12). As far as Jesus was concerned, being single is not only good, it's a gift from God.

Paul also agreed. When certain Corinthians wrote asking whether or not it's "good for a man not to marry" (1 Cor. 7:1), Paul replied that for some, it was better to be single—it was better for him—and, in concert with Jesus, he declared that celibacy was a gift from God: "I wish that all men were as I am [single]. But each man has his own gift from God; one has this gift, another has that" (7:7).

So I ask you now, would Jesus and His apostles teach us that singleness is a gift of God if it's a serious impediment to one's pursuit of satisfaction in Him? Of course not! If you're called to be single, you're not strange; you're someone very special.

Paul, in this same context, elaborates on the greater advantages of being single. Since we're all here a short time, he concludes, being single means that we can make the most of our time: "What I mean, brothers, is that the time is short. . . . This world in its present form is passing away. I would like you to be free from concern. An unmarried man is concerned about the Lord's affairs—how he can please the Lord" (7:29–32).

It does seem downright un-American for single people, who have so much discretionary time and money, not to go for the loudest stereo and the quickest car they can buy. But such an outlook for God's men and women seems tawdry and cheap compared to a life lived out for His good. The greater advantage of the solitary life is that one has unfettered opportunity to invest a life in eternal things.

Could Paul have won the West if he had taken "a believing wife along . . . , as do the other apostles and the Lord's brothers and Cephas" (1 Cor. 9:5)? Paul himself insists that if one marries, he or she must be devoted to marriage, but, as Paul points out, the unmarried person is concerned solely about the Lord's affairs (7:34).

One problem with being single is that you're always in transit, always waiting for the wedding so you can get on with your life. One of my unmarried friends described the feeling this way: "The suggestion creeps into my mind that I'm incomplete; I'm in a holding pattern, flying around trying to find an airport so I can get my feet on the ground and start living. It comes up even in the way I live, the way I place things in my room. I keep thinking, 'When I have my own place . . . ,' or 'When I have someone with me, then I'll do this or that. . . .' This kind of thinking keeps me from being the man God has called me to be right now" (John Fischer).

Singleness can be viewed as an olive jammed in the neck of a bottle—the one impediment that frustrates the use of one's giftedness. Thus when a person gets singleness out of the system, the rest of the person will come out. But it must not be so; we must bloom where we're planted. Our call to Christ sanctifies every state, even the single state. God's grace is sufficient for now!

Paul observes that it's not being married that ends a person's woes: "Those who marry will face many troubles in this life"—neither the married nor the single state will do ultimately (7:28). Francis Bacon wrote,

Domestic cares afflict the husband's bed,
    Or pain his head.
Those that live single take it for a curse,
    Some would have children;
Those that have them moan or wish them gone.
    What is it then to have or have no wife,
But single thraldom or double strife.

In the end, only God will do.

Being single doesn't mean that your urge to merge will diminish, nor does it mean that you won't be lonely and sometimes sad; being single with God simply means that you won't be alone. As Paul himself learned, you can "remain" (live by yourself) with God (7:24).

BURNOUT

Warm-up: Numbers 11:1–15

God will speak to this people, to
whom he said, "This is the resting
place, let the weary rest"; and
"This is the place of repose"
—but they would not listen (Isa. 28:12).

So you're feeling a little down or simply old and spent. Consider Moses. He also wanted to quit.

You know the story: "The rabble with them began to crave other food, and again the Israelites started wailing and said, 'If only we had meat to eat! We remember the fish we ate in Egypt at no cost—also the cucumbers, melons, leeks, onions and garlic. But now we have lost our appetite; we never see anything but this manna' " (Num. 11:4–6). Manna was the "grain of heaven," (Ps. 78:24), but God's people wanted more—more than God had given.

It was too much for Moses! He unraveled: "Why have you brought this trouble on your servant?" he asked God angrily. "Where can I get meat for all these people? They keep wailing to me, 'Give us meat to eat!' I cannot carry all these people by myself; the burden is too heavy for me. If this is how you are going to treat me, put me to death right now—if I have found favor in your eyes—and do not let me face my own ruin" (Num. 11:11, 13–15).

This was the man who once stood up to the most

powerful ruler of his day, who plagued Egypt, parted the Red Sea, brought Israel through the wilderness to Sinai, and gave them the Law. But all at once he came to the end of his rope—stressed out by too much to do and by too many people with too many problems.

His burnout was classic, the result of thinking that everything depended on him. He thought he must carry all the burdens of ministry on his shoulders because there were no other shoulders.

He began to worry about the future and how he would ever feed his crowd. Over-extended and emotionally overloaded, Moses began to brood over his inadequacy and potential for failure. He got angry and resentful at God's people and then at God Himself, collapsing into self-pity, depression, and self-destructive thoughts.

The problem with Moses was that he was taking too much on himself, doing far more than God ever intended him to do. No one ever sank under the burden of God's will. It's when we run ahead of Him and add our will to His that we get beyond our strength. If we find ourselves so loaded we should at least remember that it's our own doing and not His.

Furthermore, Moses was taking too much thought for tomorrow, adding that burden to the burden of today, a weight that's more than anyone can bear. As Jesus said, we shouldn't "worry about tomorrow, for tomorrow will worry about itself. Each day has enough trouble of its own" (Matt. 6:34). God doesn't tax us with tomorrow. He rather "leaves us to leave the future to him, and mind the present" (George MacDonald).

But Moses did the essential thing: He took his overload to God. Israel complained *about* God and got

nowhere; Moses complained *to* God and received mercy
(11:16–30).

God can handle our scoldings. In fact, our outbursts
of resentment and rage at Him are often the first step
toward recovery. Though our anger is initially turned
against God, at least it turns us to Him.

So it was with Moses, whose distress put him back in
touch with God, where he received the comfort and
counsel he needed to carry on. He learned about sharing
the burden of responsibility with others (11:16–25), but
more important, he was reminded of God's sufficiency
in all of his circumstances: "Is the LORD's arm too
short?" God asked. "*Wait* and see!" (11:23, paraphrase).

Most of us are too busy to wait for God. We have
things to do, "and promises to keep, and miles to go
before we sleep" (Robert Frost). We over-dose on
everything; we get caught up in the system, commit
ourselves to projects and plans that God never intended
for us, and then wonder how we can ever get them done.

A person can't fight the demons of busyness directly;
they're much too strong. Our only hope is to wait for
God.

Waiting on Him each day helps us to recall His
adequacy. We're reminded that we "can do everything
through him who gives [us] strength" (Phil. 4:13).
Though we may feel incompetent, "such confidence as
this is ours through Christ before God" (2 Cor. 3:4). The
demands on us are actually demands upon Him. That
confidence gives us poise in the face of intense pressure.

Furthermore, waiting on Him enables us to know
what He wants us to do each day. We're delivered from
that feeling that everything depends on us—that if we

don't do what should be done it won't get done. We're reminded that He has others through whom can He work. He can in fact raise up servants from asses and stones if necessary.

And so we need a time and place each day to wait on God, gain His outlook again, and get His agenda for each day; a time just for the two of us where we can talk over His business and our busyness with Him; a place from which we can experience God's presence and purpose through the day.

A friend of mine suggested a helpful analogy. He said that our busy lives are a lot like trying to stay on a playground merry-go-round: The closer one is to the center, the easier it is to hold on. The center—God's quiet presence—is the resting place for His hyperactive servants.

OLD-TIMERS

Warm-up: 1 Kings 12:1–17

*Rehoboam rejected the advice the elders gave him
and consulted [instead] the young men who had
grown up with him (1 Kings 12:8).*

Jake was old. His legs were thin and bowed; they
seemed much too spindly to hold him against the
current of the Deschutes River. His waders looked older
still: They were discolored, cracked, and patched. His
fishing vest was jerry-rigged with safety pins; his
ancient cowboy hat was battered and sweat-stained. His
antiquated fiberglass fly rod was scarred and taped. He
was hardly state-of-the-art.

I watched bemused as he worked his way upstream
into a patch of quiet water and began to cast. And then I
really took notice! He was fishing water I'd fished earlier,
putting his fly over pockets I'd missed, taking trout
where I'd caught none. Here was a man who could teach
me a thing or two! Emerson was right: "Every man is my
superior in some way. In that I can learn from him."

And so I ask myself, "Where can I find some old-
timer who is my superior in the Word, who knows God
as I want to know Him; where is that spiritual director
and counselor in whom I can find security?"

They're somewhat uncommon, but they are surely
there, and we must find them. God leaves none of us
without witness. Everyone can teach us a little, but

77

occasionally there are older, wiser souls in whom we can trust and from whom we can learn much. These sages are our safety. We've got to find them, cultivate their friendship, and hear what they have to say.

As Thomas à Kempis said, "Who is so wise as to be able to know all things? Therefore, trust not too much in your own thoughts, but be willing also to hear the sentiments of others. . . . It is more safe to hear and take counsel than to give it. It may happen that one's thought may be good; but to refuse to yield to others, when reason or just cause requires it, is a sign of pride and willfulness."

The ability to listen to one's elders is unnatural, but it's a quality that has to be learned, and sometimes it's learned the hard way.

I think of Rehoboam, Solomon's son and the successor to his throne. You would expect some of Solomon's famous wisdom to have rubbed off on the young man, but unfortunately, as Solomon aged and edged away from God the old king made a fool of himself.

One of his worst mistakes was to conscript Israelites as slave labor to build "the LORD's temple, his own palace, the supporting terraces, the wall of Jerusalem, and Hazor, Megiddo and Gezer. . . . He built up Lower Beth Horon, Baalath, and Tadmor . . . as well as all his store cities and the towns for his chariots and for his horses . . ." (1 Kings 9:15–19).

It would have been one thing to build a national sanctuary—an exceptional work that would have galvanized his people and enlisted their sympathies—but it was another to coerce them into building projects that served only to aggrandize the king. That unwelcome chore created widespread dissatisfaction and several times brought Israel to the edge of civil war. And so, when Solomon died and a new order emerged, the tribes from the north and their would-be leader, Jeroboam, appealed to Rehoboam for relief: "Your father put a heavy yoke on us, but now lighten the harsh labor . . . , and we will serve you" (1 Kings 12:4).

Rehoboam was nonplussed. He asked for time to consider their request and then consulted the elders who had served his father: " 'How would you advise me to answer these people?' he asked. They replied, 'If today you will be a servant to these people and serve them and give them a favorable answer, they will always be your servants' " (12:6–7).

The elders gave sound advice—good leaders should lead by compassion and not by fear—but Rehoboam "rejected the advice the elders gave him and consulted [instead] the young men who had grown up with him and were serving him. He asked them, 'What is your advice? How should we answer these people?' " The young men replied, "Tell them, 'My little finger is thicker than my father's waist. My father laid on you a heavy yoke; I will make it even heavier. My father scourged you with whips; I will scourge you with scorpions [a type of whip with iron hooks]' " (12:10–11).

And so, taking the counsel of his young friends, Rehoboam began his reign by cracking his whip, but his gambit failed. Jeroboam and his followers walked out, Israel seceded from Judah and crowned Jeroboam as their king. Rehoboam had single-handedly torn the nation apart—a schism from which they never recovered—all because he forsook the advice of his elders and listened instead to his peers.

As I thought about this foolishness a principle emerged: When in doubt, ask an old grizzly. All of us need the counsel of older, wiser folks. (In my case, it's time for me to find an even older grizzly.)

Of course not all old-timers are wise. There are wise old folks and there are wicked old folks, and some men and women just get to be old fools. But since all knowledge, wisdom, and character is cumulative, it follows that those who have loved the Savior a long time will reach maturity rich in their understanding of God and be wise in His ways. Think of the calm He brings, the understanding He leaves them, "the hoarded spoils, the legacies of time."

Old-timers who have walked a long time with God and have listened well to His counsel usually have something to say. It's good to seek them out and heed their counsel. In a multitude of such counselors, there is safety (Prov. 11:14).

PERSISTENCE THAT PAYS

Warm-up: 1 Corinthians 4:1–13

Many a man claims to have unfailing love,
but a faithful man who can find? (Prov. 20:6).

Some of my friends are steelhead fishermen, which means, of course, that I'm occasionally obliged to join them in their pursuit of that wily game-fish. I always do it against my better judgment.

The question comes to me, standing waist-deep in icy water, dodging ice floes and trying to cast a fly line into the teeth of gale-force winds, Why would any creature with an IQ higher than a slab of concrete want to do this to himself, particularly when he hardly ever catches a fish? They tell me steelheaders average one fish every twenty hours or so. I'm the guy who brings the average down for the whole crowd. However, as they say, once you catch a steelhead, life is never the same!

I'll say this for steelheaders: They are persistent! Good steelhead fishermen never give up. They have a Job-like patience that puts the rest of the world to shame. So, as in most good pursuits, patience and persistence are the name of the game.

Once upon a time we believed that nothing worthwhile came easily. Today, it's assumed that almost anything ought to be done quickly and with very little effort. In such a world it isn't hard to get started, but it sure is hard to endure for very long. When the novelty wears off, our interest wears thin. There's a market for all kinds of experience, but little enthusiasm for the patient acquisition of anything arduous; little inclination to sign up for anything that's long-term and hard.

But being authentically Christian is often just a matter of making hard choices and sticking with them because we know that what God asks is for our good. "The essential thing," as Friedrich Nietzsche said, "is that there should be a long obedience in the same direction; there thereby results, and has always resulted in the long run, something which has made life worth living."

Real Christianity means giving ourselves to everyday, low-profile obedience—an activity for which we get the least encouragement from our hustling peers. Other people initially have more flash; they are euphoric whirlwinds of activity as long as things go well. But then they encounter pain and resistance, and they fold. They are sensual people—governed by feelings rather than by the Word.

What's required of us, on the other hand, is dogged determined, endurance, keeping at the task of following Jesus through life's ebbs and flows, ups and downs, whether we feel like it or not, knowing that it's God "who works in [us] to will and to act according to his good purpose" (Phil. 2:13). We won't get everything right—we're only human—but God sees the heart and knows its intent, and He encourages every effort to comply. He's dogged in His endurance too, and wonderfully persistent. He never gives up on us.

Paul said, "It is required that those who have been given a trust must prove faithful" (1 Cor. 4:2). Not always successful. Just faithful. It is necessary then that we keep showing up, willing to do what our Lord is asking us to do, however difficult it may be. Slowly, staunchly, steadfastly—that's how every hard task is finally done.

Woody Allen was right: "Eighty percent of life is just showing up."

THE BREAKING

Warm-up: Genesis 32:22–32

*. . . as a man he struggled
with God (Hos. 12:3).*

Jacob was born gripping his twin brother's heel, holding his brother back, trying to get ahead. Therefore he was named *Jacob—heeler* in Hebrew.

True to his name, Jacob hustled his way through life wheeling and dealing, trying to trip others up to get a head start, knowing God, but not needing him very much. He had his own ways of getting things done. But he met his match when he met the "Man," the night he wrestled with God.

The wrestling match came after a day of frenzied ambivalence, praying and plotting, trusting God and trying on his own. Years before, Jacob had swindled his brother Esau out of his birthright and inheritance, and now they were about to meet. That night, in the anxious hours before their meeting, when Jacob was all alone, "a man wrestled with him till daybreak" (Gen. 32:24).

Jacob and the stranger brawled through the night, pounding and punishing each other, rolling in the dust, a fall to one and then the other. When dawn approached and the "Man" saw that Jacob would not surrender, "he touched the socket of Jacob's hip so that his hip was wrenched as he wrestled" (32:25). Jacob's antagonist made a move that crippled him.

Jacob, expended, couldn't go on; he could only clench. "Let me go," his opponent shouted. But Jacob continued to cling. " 'I will not let you go unless you bless me.' The man asked him, 'What is your name?' 'Jacob,' he answered. Then the man said, 'Your name will no longer be Jacob, but Israel [one who prevails with God], because you have struggled with God and with men and have overcome.' " (Gen. 32:26–28).

Phantom match or real encounter? Jacob knew. His opponent was God Himself, coming to grips with Jacob's duplicity, wrestling with him, relentless in His love. He would not give up until Jacob gave in and made God's will his own.

This clash was the climax of Jacob's life-long ambivalence, fighting God and yet clinging to Him. And now, utterly defeated, exhausted, at last, Jacob gave up his fight with God and gave in.

Jacob knew who he was—schemer and dreamer—but old Jacob was finished. He could no longer survive except with a vice-like grip on God, clinging to Him and counting on Him. The old "Jacob" was a new man. He was now "Israel"—a man who had struggled with God and prevailed. Defeat and victory had come at the same time. God had grappled with Jacob, thoroughly broken him, and Jacob had won!

"So Jacob called the place Peniel, saying, '. . . I saw God face to face, and yet my life was spared.' The sun rose above him as he passed Peniel, and he was limping because of his hip" (32:30–31). Jacob went on disabled, ever after dragging his leg. But the sun was rising on a new day and on a new life for the man whom God had subdued and saved.

Jacob's story is ours. We too want God, but not too much. And so we wrestle with Him—relying on Him and yet resisting Him. He then becomes our adversary. Because He is for us He pits His strength against us, bringing us down. Our dreams don't materialize, our schemes won't work, our co-workers disappoint us, our ministries fail.

He does not bring such evil upon us—He cannot be the source—but He permits it to come. This is the "Man" who dusts us up and brings us down, breaking our hearts to bring us home.

> Well mayest thou then work on indocile hearts;
> By small successes, disappointments small;
> By nature, weather, failure or sore fall;
> By shame, anxiety, bitterness and smarts;
> By loneliness, by weary loss of zest.
> The rags, the husks, the swine, the hunger quest,
> Drive home the wanderer to the Father's breast.
> —George MacDonald

Jacob's maiming marked him forever. But if you could ask him about his affliction, he would have said that the climax of his life was that terrible night when God finally pinned him to the mat. That was the night Jacob lost and finally won.

CREDIBILITY

You are the salt of the earth. . . .
You are the light of the world
(Matt. 5:13–14).

Jesus' assertion that the church is the earth's salt and light sounds audacious in a society where so few take church-going seriously anymore. But He said it: God's people are the element that arrests the spread of corruption in the world; we alone are the substance that dispels illusion and its offspring, despair. The church is still the only agent in society that can cleanse the world and correct the lies that debase it.

By "church" I do not mean, of course, the buildings, programs, and professionals of the church. I'm thinking rather of individual believers who are examples of authentic belief and who are committed to making visible to the world the invisible Jesus. The real business of the church is done by men and women whose inner lives are characterized by truth, righteousness, humility, and servanthood, and who love each other as He loves us, with a fierce and determined love.

Church-goers like this have a profound effect on the unchurched. Therefore, we should see that the heart of our mission is to "say 'No' to ungodliness . . . and to live self-controlled, upright and godly lives in this present age," as Paul put it (Titus 2:12). That's what it

87

means to be salt and light in the world and that's the only way the world will ever be saved. The best wooing and winning of the lost, therefore, is done by those who are busy doing the real business of the church.

The devil wants to thwart that business if he can. That's why we often have a hard time in the most unexpected place—within the church itself. That's why we sometimes rub each other the wrong way and even committed Christians have problems getting along. If you were the devil and wanted to subvert God's plan to salvage the world, whom would you try to trip up? The agents, of course, by whom He plans to save it.

Karl Marx taught his agents "The Way of the Fox"— subtle subversion rather than sudden takeover. The way to overthrow a people, he said, is to first penetrate (worm in) and then indoctrinate (soften up) and finally subvert (win over). It sounded diabolical at the time—too devilish even for Marx. But I think he got the idea from the devil himself, who has been at it from the beginning.

Satan penetrates by finding willing agents within the church—naive, unthinking believers whom he can manipulate and use. Then he indoctrinates, suggesting ungodly ways and means of dealing with their difficulties with one another. He makes them want to be noticed; they get hurt when they're overlooked; they smart when they're crossed, corrected, or criticized; they harbor grudges, nurse grievances, and wallow in self-pity; they gossip about others and blame them for their pain rather than see God's hand in all things. They choose their own kind rather than the lowly and the unlovely. They insist on being the center of attention rather than serving out on the edge.

It happens all the time! Those who are seduced forget that God was once a lamb—that He overcame injustice by humility and meekness. They forget about giving up their rights to control things and be in charge, about loving those who don't love them, as our Lord did. Unlike Him, they look for the inside track and special favor. They search for selfish advantage rather than someone to serve. They forget what it means to be concealed and content, without praise or notice; to be undervalued and sometimes slighted. They forget that little things can mean a lot. Relationships break down, the church begins to break up, and our influence on the world is gone.

It occurs to me that Satan's strategy must be to get a church to go bad from within so God Himself must judge it. Jesus told John that when a church loses it's saltiness He would eventually have to remove its lampstand (Rev. 2:5). The people may gather, the piano may play, the preacher may pray, but the lights are out. It happens all the time. God forbid that we should be ignorant of Satan's devices.

CHANGING MINDS

Warm-up: 2 Timothy 2:23–26

The Lord's servant must not quarrel;
instead, he must be kind to everyone,
able to teach, not resentful (2 Tim. 2:24).

Agatha Christie said of Meadowbrook School and its presiding spirit, Miss Bulstrode, "There was discipline there without regimentation," by which she meant that learning took place in an atmosphere of empathy and understanding. I read that sentence a few weeks ago and my mind went back to Mamie, who taught me how to paint.

Carolyn and I first met Mamie in Montana and marveled at her artistry. She worked wonders on canvas. She made us want to paint. She volunteered one day to teach us: "Anyone can learn to paint," she said. "I can help you; won't you come to my class?" We showed up the next day, eager to learn.

Mamie taught with kindness; she created a loving climate for learning. Some in her class did better than others—some are just naturally better—but she never depreciated anyone's effort; she praised every attempt to get the hang of things and make it better.

She didn't get angry when we botched our painting, though she did expect compliance. She could be quite stern. "No! No!" she'd say, "You're getting it all wrong!"

And then she'd point to her picture. "Do it like this," she'd insist. We knew she just wanted us to get it right.

If we did go wrong, she'd paint over our mistakes and encourage us to start again. Or in some difficult place, she'd place her hand over ours and guide our strokes until they became like hers. And in the end she praised us all and displayed our works for all to see. Mamie gently taught us how to paint. There was discipline there without regimentation.

Mamie's approach to her students reminds me of the kindly spirit of the apostle Paul when he wrote, "The Lord's servant must not quarrel; instead, he must be kind to everyone, able to teach, not resentful. Those who oppose him he must gently instruct, in the hope that God will grant them repentance leading them to a knowledge of the truth, and that they will come to their senses and escape from the trap of the devil, who has taken them captive to do his will" (2 Tim. 2:24–26).

It's a sin to bully people—to be combative and argumentative. Discussion and debate on the facts is one thing; assault is another. When we resort to coercion we've already lost our moral and rational force. The Puritans were right when they enunciated the principle of consent. Faith can never be foisted on another. Consent must be gained by gentle persuasion and reason rather than mandate. People are best charmed into compliance.

So we should avoid what Paul calls "foolish and stupid arguments" (2:23) and always be "kind to everyone"—intelligent and relevant in our proclamation and nondefensive in our posture, gently instructing those who oppose, "in the hope that God will grant them repentance . . . that they may come to their senses and escape from the trap of the devil who has taken them captive to do his will" (2:24–26).

Those who oppose are not the enemy but victims of the enemy, deceived and captured by him to do his will. They may be delivered, Paul insists, but only if we speak the truth in love.

Truth alone is never enough. Without love it is mere dogma and it never touches the soul. And without truth, love becomes mere sentimentalism. Only truth delivered with lovingkindness has power to change another's mind. Truth sounds good only when it's spoken with courtesy.

The best teachers thus are never ill-mannered or ironfisted. Our Lord showed us the way: "Take my yoke upon you and *learn from me*, for I am gentle and humble in heart . . ." (Matt. 11:29–30, emphasis added).

THE LITTLE ONES

Warm-up: Matthew 18:1–14

Let the little children come to me,
and do not hinder them . . . (Luke 18:16).

I wandered into the boy's restroom on the back hall the other day. I'm seldom in that part of our building during the school day, since the place is normally over-run with little children.

I peeked into the boy's room and spied a tearful youngster standing in the middle of the floor, holding up his trousers with both hands.

"Hi!" I said, trying to be jovial. "What's up?" It was the wrong question to ask or the wrong way to ask it. His reaction was to look even more desperate. "What's the matter?" I tried again. "Are you having a hard time with school?" "Yes!" he sobbed. "Why?" I asked. "Cause I can't get my pants snapped!" he wailed. I came to his rescue and sent him on his way. Suddenly everything seemed much better—for me as well as for him.

The incident set me to thinking about little children: How easily their needs can be met; how tragic it is when we adults fail to meet them. It's the little things that count: listening to them while they chatter; looking intently into their eyes when we speak; affirming their value and worth; correcting them gently when they err;

showering them with kindness; assuring them that we care; calming them with tenderness and touch; and most of all, giving them something other than E. T. to hold onto—showing them the glorious attractiveness of Jesus, and helping them on to God.

Children are wonderfully credulous. Jesus said they were. He referred to the street urchins of His day, who constantly pestered Him and annoyed His disciples no end, as "these little ones who believe in me." He corrected His older followers for trying to shoo them away and recommended to His disciples that they grow up and become like children in child-like faith. In fact, according to Jesus, we must all become like children if we plan to enter the kingdom of heaven (Mark 10:15). We should, as someone observed, get over our childish fears, including our fear of being childish.

Time and misfortune make cynics of us, but little children just naturally believe. They often grasp the deep things of God's Word, even though those mysteries are so deep that not even an adult can fathom them fully. As one early Christian observed, the Bible is a river in which little lambs can wade while elephants flounder.

Childhood decides. It's the season of the soul, the prime time to plant for a lifetime.

What a privilege we have to share in the growing of a child.

THE PRUNING

Warm-up: John 15:1–11

Every branch that does bear fruit he prunes
so that it will be even more fruitful (John 15:2).

The frost got our grapes this week—sorry-looking things, all dead and dying. But then I suppose they weren't much use all along. Though green and luxuriant, they grew only a few grapes. I failed to cut them back last year.

Mere growth is never enough; productivity is the thing, and every organism has to be cut back to be fruitful. The ancient vine-dresser pruned his branches so they would produce more fruit. Sometimes, it seems, we too have to be cut back, almost to nothing. It isn't always the dead and ugly branches that have to go either (we're glad to be rid of those), but the living and vital must be put to death that a better and more bountiful thing may grow.

Paul once pointed out that "we who are alive are always being given over to death for Jesus' sake, so that his life may be revealed in our mortal body" (2 Cor. 4:11). It seems we're always being delivered up—to the cheap shots, the hurts, and the hard things that cut us to the heart. But the knife that cuts is in fact a pruning knife, putting an end to our life so that in the end we may be what we ought to be—living memorials of Jesus.

A Burden Shared

The pruning knife is that rejecting gesture, that unkind or critical word, or no word at all, for me the most painful cut of all. It's losing out—when another gets in our way, or always seems to get his or her way. It's living in a constant state of noise and confusion, with daily pedestrian duties and no chance or choice to find a quiet place to call our own. It's waiting—hope deferred—with no promised togetherness, no companionship, no liberation, no end of waiting in sight.

But the pruning knife is guided by a pair of good hands. The cuts only rid us of extraneous growth; the dying is necessary. And those who lose their lives reap a harvest of character and influence on others. The Vine-dresser knows what we can take, and He dreams of what we can be—more loving, joyful, tranquil, tolerant, kindly, dependable, gentle, poised, and strong.

He has to get on with it and we have to go on. There's no going on without the cutting back. Take comfort from the knife; trust the hands that hold it and submit to them, looking on to the harvest. You can count on it: The fruit is always good!

RUNNING AWAY

Warm-up: Jeremiah 9:1–26

Oh, that I had in the desert a lodging
place for travelers, so that I might
leave my people and go away from
them (Jer. 9:2).

Sometimes, I think Jeremiah had it exactly right. He wanted a cabin in the woods where he could get away from it all. He was fed up with folks; he'd had it. He wanted out—way out—away from them all.

I get the feeling myself from time to time—the yen to get a job in a lighthouse or drop out and build a log cabin with my own hands, way up in the mountains and let the world go to pieces. Deep down I just want to be left alone.

It's a pervasive fantasy. William Yeats felt the urge: "I will arise now and go to Innisfree, / And a small cabin build there, of clay and wattles made; / Nine bean rows will I have there, a hive for the honey bee, / And live alone in the bee-loud glade."

King David did too: "Oh, that I had the wings of a dove," he cried, "I would fly away and be at rest—I would flee far away and stay in the desert; I would hurry to my place of shelter, far from the tempest and storm" (Ps. 55:6–8).

I think everybody must get that inclination now and then. Genesis says that it's not good to be alone, but honestly, sometimes being alone sounds like the best thing in the world.

I get tired of the hassles, the responsibilities, the everlasting demands, the people, wall to wall. There is no end of things to be done for others. I get weary of doing things for them and hearing about their worries and woes.

It's then that I begin to dream about dropping out and going away.

But it won't do. Final escape is a fantasy and fantasy has no place in our lives. We're to be girded about with reality (Eph. 6:14).

We can't drop out. There's more at stake than our own solace.

That's why the word came to Jeremiah from the Lord: "Proclaim all these words in the *towns* of Judah and in the *streets* of Jerusalem. 'Listen to the terms of this covenant and follow them' " (Jer. 11:6, emphasis added).

Jeremiah couldn't stay in the high country; he had to go back to town. There were things to be done, the word to be proclaimed, people to be helped on to God.

Raphael's alter piece in the Vatican depicts Jesus on the Mountain of Transfiguration with the three disciples, James, Peter, and John. All is light and glory. At the foot of the mountain all is gloom and doom. The disciples want to remain on the mountain top, but Jesus won't let them stay. They have to come down with Him and live in the world of darkness and demons, down where the redemptive rubber meets the road.

It's necessary to go to the mountains and get away now and then; "Great things are done when men and mountains meet; / This is not done by jostling in the street" (William Blake). We should by all means find some time to be alone and get away from the crowds, if only for a few hours each week. We need a quiet place in which to rest and in which God can recreate our love for Him and refresh our souls. The mountain renews us as it renewed our Lord. He often went into the mountains so there would be nothing between Him and God (cf. Luke 6:12).

But, though solitude is a good place to visit, it's no place to stay. God says to us what he said to Jeremiah, "Proclaim all these words in the *towns* . . . and in the *streets.*"

TABLE TALK

Warm-up: Luke 19:1–10

*The Son of Man came to seek
and to save what was lost
(Luke 19:10).*

I am fascinated by Zacchaeus—the dwarfish man who hung from the limb of a tree to see Jesus, trying to rise above the crowd. He was obviously looking for something.

Zacchaeus was a long-time district tax commissioner, a quisling who had purchased the Jericho tax franchise from the Romans and who encumbered his neighbors to make himself rich. He had sold out to the evil empire and thus, in the eyes of his countrymen, had sold his soul to the devil.

The clergy also considered him too far gone. He had forsaken "the way of the Law" and was on his way to Gehenna. He was a long lost soul.

But Jesus picked him out of the crowd—there was no censure or condescension—and invited Himself over for lunch. He said, " 'Zacchaeus, come down immediately. I must stay at your house today.' So he came down at once and welcomed him gladly" (Luke 19:5–6).

Jesus' self-invitation sounds rude and presumptuous to us, but in the culture of that day it was a gesture of acceptance. You only ate and drank with people you preferred; Zacchaeus took it that Jesus wanted to be his friend.

One of the distinctive features of Jesus' ministry was His inclination to eat and drink with sinners even though it made Him scandalous and dangerous to the clergy of His day. The immediate and unthinkable conclusion was that God was the friend of riffraff. And, as it turns out, He is! As Jesus said, "The Son of Man came to seek and to save what was *lost*" (19:10, emphasis added).

Jesus never expects anyone to apply more spit and polish to get to Him. He just wants men and women to sit down with Him at His table. But there is something about sitting down with Jesus that improves one's manners. Listening to Him, watching Him, and waiting on Him makes you want to be like Him. After a while you take on His likeness.

So Zacchaeus, when he heard Jesus' offer, came down out of his tree to sit with Him and listen to Him, and later rose from the table to say, "Look, Lord! Here and now I give half of my possessions to the poor, and if I have cheated anybody out of anything, I will pay back four times the amount" (19:8).

Zacchaeus, who knew his own short-fall, had long compensated for his smallness with ill-gotten wealth. It was his only refuge from despair. But now he no longer needed his sinful resort. He had sought out and found the One who could help him stand tall.

Jesus said, "Today salvation has come to this house, because this man, too, is a son of Abraham." The outsider had been brought in; the Son of Man had saved what was lost.

If you sit at Jesus' table you never know with whom you'll be sitting. "The soldier who occupies your country shares your cup. The tax collector who never fails to knock on your door on the first of the month eats bread with you" (John Shea). The new answer to the old question, "Who is my brother and sister?" becomes in Jesus, "Whomever Jesus is seeking; whoever sits down with Him."

Idolaters, adulterers, prostitutes, homosexuals, thieves, slanderers, and swindlers become our kind of people. We can't pick our companions any more. We're *all* the lost He came to save.

IN PRAISE OF THE SMALL

Warm-up: Haggai 2:1–9

How does it look to you now? Does it not
seem to you like nothing? (Hag. 2:3).

The little structure seemed like nothing compared to Solomon's magnificent temple. Those who were engaged in building it were mostly farmers, with little time to invest in labor and no money with which to hire professionals. It was a do-it-yourself project, pieced together by local effort.

The workers were faithful and were forging on, but the building still wasn't much to look at—no gold, silver, or precious stones. Those who had seen the glory of Solomon's eight-million dollar building sat down and wept.

That's when Haggai spoke up:

"Who of you is left who saw this house in its former glory? How does it look to you now? Does it not seem to you like nothing? But now be strong . . . all you people of the land," declares the LORD, "and work. For I am with you," declares the LORD Almighty. . . . "My Spirit remains among you. Do not fear." This is what the LORD Almighty says: "In a little while I will once more shake the heavens and the earth, the sea and the dry land. I will shake all nations, and the desired one of all nations will come, and I will fill this house with glory," says the LORD Almighty (2:3–7).

And He did. This little house, embellished by Herod, was the temple to which Jesus came, filling it with His glory. There's no end of good that God can do with a very small thing.

"Who despises the day of small things?" asks one of Haggai's contemporaries (Zech. 4:10). We do! Small has fallen on hard times, inclined as we are to equate size with success. Small is now a value judgment: If we're little we're limited or worth nothing at all.

We know in theory that it's "not by might nor power but by God's spirit" that God's work is done, and yet in practice we keep counting noses and falling short and feeling that what we're doing is insignificant. "We have become fascinated by the idea of bigness, and we are quite convinced that if we could only stage, yes, that's the word, stage something really big before the world, we would shake it and produce a mighty religious awakening" (Martin Lloyd-Jones).

But what is highly valued among men is detested by God (Luke 16:15). He delights in smallness, and always seems to do His best work through a tiny remnant, like Gideon's army, whom God dismantled, reducing it from 22,000 to 300 because, as he said, "You have too many men for me" (Judg. 7:2).

No, small is not too few; it's just about right. We can be pleased when two or three are gathered in Jesus' name. Size is nothing; substance is everything. It's a matter of perspective.

A small place has fewer distractions. We can center more on the fundamentals of ministry—befriending others and imparting the truth to them.

Furthermore, everything can be simplified. We don't have to generate programs. We can gather around the piano and minister to one another in psalms and hymns and spiritual songs; we can worship around the wood stove.

A small place invites intimacy and accountability, so no one gets left out. We can know one another more fully and engage in more meaningful pastoral and mutual care.

Evangelism is doable in a little place. Community involvement is almost mandatory. Church members may participate at any level, making Christ visible to the entire community.

And from a small place we can even embrace the world. Young people leave us for the big city but if our vision is greater than our own immediate needs, we'll view their imminent departure as good news. We'll equip them with our teaching, imbue them with our vision, and send them out with our blessing to the uttermost parts of the earth—a disposition my friend Bob Smith refers to as a "boot camp mentality." (A friend told me that the tiny church in which we grew up spawned five full-time workers and one martyr while he was there).

It's all a matter of perspective. God is "able to do immeasurably more than all we ask or imagine, according to his power that is at work within us" (Eph. 3:20).

Oh, to be sure, there are challenges in small places,

but they come not from smallness of place but from smallness of mind—short-sightedness, traditionalism, legalism, and the other cramping carnalities that initially frustrate God's purposes and leave us dismayed.

But we don't have to push such people over the edge. Our strength lies not in stubbornness and forcefulness but in speaking the truth in love—patient, long-term instruction from God's Word, humbly and prayerfully offered, "in the hope that . . . they will come to their senses and escape from the trap of the devil who has taken them captive to do his will" (2 Tim. 2:25–26).

In due time God may work on the most rigid of them, softening their hard hearts and minds and setting them free to do His will.

And so I say, we don't have to move on. We can be content where we are. We all get a yen now and then to move up to a bigger place, but to be true to the gospel we should rather choose to move down (Luke 14:7–11). Upward mobility may be the American way, but it's not necessarily God's way for His own. True nobility is a matter of moving down the ladder, seeking to be the servant of all.

God may thrust us out—"extrude" us, to use Francis Schaeffer's colorful term. Some of us will get sacked; others will have to leave because we cannot provide for our families. In some cases we, like our Lord, will be unable to do any mighty works because of the hardness of folk's hearts. God has many ways to move us to another, perhaps larger site. But if we *grasp* for the bigger place we'll not be effective there. Grasping is sin. "Should you then seek great things for yourself?" Jeremiah asks. "Seek them not!" (Jer. 45:5). The higher seats "belong to those for whom they have been prepared" (Mark 10:40). In the meantime it's best to stay put as long as it pleases God—if it be His will, until we die.

Longevity means a lot: It matures us, deepening our devotion to Christ, making us more like Him than we ever thought possible and preparing us for a lifetime of service wherever He calls us. The fish-bowl effect of small communities demands authentic Christianity. If we move too fast we may never deal with flaws that must be addressed. Remaining is a character-building move.

Moreover, remaining matures our ministry. It's been my experience that nothing much happens for five to ten years. That's when the hireling is inclined to flee. But a good shepherd sticks it out, quietly manifesting Jesus' love, patiently tending God's flock, faithfully serving his neighbors—no matter how long it takes or how much it costs—until God makes His move.

Some churches will never get bigger. In a small, static community there are ceilings to growth. But there's no limit to spiritual growth. People can grow in grace forever. Every day we remain is a step closer to their maturity. As one of the early church Fathers said, "If you happen to live in a community do not move to another place, for it will harm you greatly. If a bird leaves her eggs they will never hatch."

The bottom line for me is just to know that serving in a small place is not a stepping stone to greatness. It *is* greatness.

SEXUAL SUICIDE

Warm-up: Proverbs 5:1–23

*Why be captivated, my son, by an
adulteress? Why embrace the
bosom of another man's wife?
(Prov. 5:20).*

I keep seeing my friends fall. I wonder why they do it?
What causes men and women to trash their marriages
for a transient affair? Why would we give our strength
to others and fill our old age with regret (Prov. 5:9)?

Perhaps it's naiveté. We think we're invincible, like
Samson,

> man of giant strength—
> [who] pillowed his great head upon
> the lap of sin
> then rose at length
> "not knowing
> that his strength was gone."
> —Ruth Bell Graham

Samson was a fool and so are we if we believe that we
will never fall. Everyone is temptable; everyone has a
price. The key is to know how vulnerable we are and
always be on the alert. We're overthrown because we're
unguarded (1 Cor. 10:12). "What can we do?" we ask.

We can guard our relationship with God. As the
proverb says, "Above all else, guard your heart, for it is

the wellspring of life" (Prov. 4:23). There's a close relationship between human sexuality and human spirituality; the two are inextricably linked. As Charles Williams noted, "Sensuality and sanctity are so closely intertwined that our motives in some cases can hardly be separated until the tares are gathered out of the wheat by heavenly wit."

Sexual passion is in some inexplicable way a small representation of our more profound, spiritual passion for God. He alone can gratify that desire. So devotion to Christ serves to satisfy our deepest longings and quell our other lusts. But when our love for Christ is on the wane, we get restless for something more and our resolve in every area begins to weaken.

We can guard our minds against romantic and sexual fantasies. "Our predominant thoughts determine our inevitable actions," as someone has said. What we think in our hearts is what we eventually do. Most moral failures aren't blowouts (hardly anyone plans an adulterous affair), but are rather like slow leaks—the result of a thousand small indulgences, the immediate consequences of which are never apparent. The small sins thus prepare us for the Big One. As Alexander Pope remarked,

> Vice is a monster of so frightful mien,
>   As to be hated needs to be seen;
> Yet seen too often, familiar with her face,
>   We first endure, then pity, then embrace.

"But," you ask, "how can we deal with our erotic thoughts?" As Philip Melanchthon learned, "Old Adam is much too strong for young Philip!" I agree. Our fantasies are much too strong to subordinate. Better to re-channel or displace them. Erotic thoughts happen, but they can be controlled. As Luther said, "We cannot keep birds from flying over our heads, but we can keep them from nesting in our hair!" When sexual fantasies intrude into our minds we have two choices: We can either reinforce them, in which case they will eventually become obsession; or we can sidetrack them into devotion, meditation, and prayer (cf. Phil. 4:8).

We men can give ourselves to being one-woman men. That's protection for both us and our spouses (cf. Prov. 5:15–16). As the wise man counseled, we should "rejoice in the wife of [our] youth . . . [and] be captivated by her love" (Prov. 5:18–19). We can work hard at cultivating intimacy in our marriages—maintaining its romance, rekindling its love and passion. Men who get in trouble usually do so because they've let their marriages drift, permitting them to become dull and unfriendly. If that's so we must woo our wives again, recapture our first love.

All of us—men and women—can watch for infatuations. St. Francis de Sales said, "We must be on guard against deception in friendships, especially when they are contracted between persons of different sexes, no matter what the pretext may be. Satan often tricks those [who] begin with virtuous love. If they are not very prudent, fond love will first be injected, next sensual love, and then carnal love. . . . [Satan] does this subtly and tries to introduce impurity by insensible degrees" (*Introduction to the Devout Life*).

It's not lust but infatuation that causes our fall. Do we think about one person frequently? Do we look for excuses to be with that individual? Do we look forward to appointments with that one? Do we dress a certain way for him or her? Most erotic relationships begin with that subtle attraction. If we find ourselves drawn to another we must go no further, not lunch nor travel nor time alone. When required to meet for business we can do so in the company of others.

We can guard against intimacy with anyone other than our spouses. The secrets of our hearts, our deepest hurts, are reserved for our mates alone. The greatest mistake we can make is to share our inner conflict and marital disappointment with someone of the opposite sex. No other event so radically shifts the nature of a relationship. We suddenly become a lonely person in need of another person's love.

Occasionally a man will meet a woman who comes after him, as the proverb puts it, dressed for the kill and "with crafty intent" (Prov. 7:10). And women are endangered by those sexual conquistadors who will tell them anything they want to hear in order to have what they want. We shouldn't kid ourselves. It's not because we're so wonderful that they love us. Such people live to bring others down; they have something to prove to themselves, or they want to see how much we'll forsake to have them. They're almost certainly acting out some terrible, inner sickness, or playing out some unresolved conflict with the opposite sex. The best course is to stay away from them! It will do us good now and then to ponder well Proverbs 5 and 7.

We can publicize our home life, talk lovingly of our mates, and surround ourselves with mementos and reminders of our marriages—pictures of our families together. It's good for us and it's good for others. It lets them know we cherish our homes.

We can regularly rehearse the consequences of an affair by asking ourselves, "Is it worth throwing away my family and my reputation for this event?"

We gain insight through hindsight, as they say, but foresight is the least expensive way to learn. As Proverbs warns, though "the lips of an adulteress drip honey, and her speech is smoother than oil; [make no mistake] in the end she is bitter as gall, sharp as a double-edged sword. Her feet go down to death; her steps lead straight to the grave" (Prov. 5:3–5). Adultery is suicidal; adulterers kill their own souls.

We can find someone who will hold us accountable—a non-judgmental friend who loves us and who won't flinch when we're honest, who will query us with the tough questions and then ask, as Howard Hendricks suggests, "In your answers to any of the above, did you lie?"

And finally, we can ask to be guarded by God every moment of the day. We're *never* safe. We're in danger whether young or old; single or married; in the dumps or on a roll. We'll never be home free until we get Home! Until then, no matter how willing the spirit, the flesh is weak. Jesus warned, "Watch and pray so that you will not fall into temptation" (Matt. 26:41).

OF DWARFS AND GIANTS

Warm-up: Proverbs 3:13–20

*I pray that you, being rooted and
established in love, may have power,
together with all the saints, to grasp
how wide and long and high and
deep is the love of Christ . . .
(Eph. 3:17–18).*

My friends tell me they have a hard time classifying
me. One told me that he thought I was either a right
wing liberal or a left wing conservative. Actually I'm
neither. I think I'm much more down the middle—
believing what most Christians have believed for the
past 2,000 years.

But I am something of an eclectic. I tend to beg,
borrow, and steal from everyone. I've been to two
seminaries, I've consorted with many kinds of believers,
I've read and listened a lot, and I've tried to learn as
much as I can.

Evangelicals have taught me to take the Scriptures
seriously. I acquired my first taste of Bible study from
them and with it an unshakable confidence in Scripture's inspiration and integrity. I've learned from some
of my liberal friends to read the Bible with more care,
seeing what's really there and understanding better the
history and culture that informs it. I think both groups
have made me more thoughtful when I study the Book.

I'm learning from Catholics about worship and devotion to Christ. Augustine, Thomas à Kempis, Teresa of Avila, Mother Teresa, St. John of the Cross, Henri Nouwen, and others have helped me to see that theology is also a matter of praise, adoration, and prayer touched off by the contemplation of God.

I've observed the dignity and power of submission and humility among the Friends—George Fox, John Woolman, Thomas Kelly, Richard Foster. They've taught me to see discipleship as persistence in contrast to the impatience of our instant age. And the Charismatics (along with Jonathan Edwards) have taught me about the place of feeling in faith. I've picked up life-forming habits from all of them.

For me it comes to this: We need others. If we would know all the dimensions of God, we must learn from *all* the saints (Eph. 3:18). Certainly, discernment is in order: Scripture must regulate and inform our thinking, and some thoughts are clearly unbiblical. Credulity is not faith but naiveté.

But on the other hand some of us are far too critical: We refuse to hear anyone who is not of our own kind. "No one quite damns like the orthodox," as they say.

We should rather "exercise the charity that rejoices in the truth wherever it is found and however unfamiliar its garb. The true Catholic, as his name implies, is the well-read, the open-minded, the hospitable-hearted, the spiritually exercised evangelical; for he belongs to all sects and all sects belong to him" (Alexander Whyte).

"Dwarfs on the shoulders of a giant . . . can see more than they . . . , because we are carried high and raised up by their giant size" (Bernard of Chartres).

THE WORD

Warm-up: 2 Timothy 3:10–17

Do your best to present yourself to God as one approved, a workman ... who correctly handles the word of truth ... (2 Tim. 2:15).

Because I take the words of Scripture seriously, I'm sometimes asked if I take them literally. (Sometimes the way the question is asked suggests these inquisitors think I still have training wheels on my bike.)

When I get the question, my stock reply is, "Why, yes, of course. Don't you?" I answer this way because I want to focus on the fact that the Bible ought to be read like any other piece of literature.

Normally, we interpret language in its plain meaning, which is what we mean when we say we take something literally. The term *literal* comes from the Latin *litera* meaning *letter*. To interpret something literally is to assume a conventional meaning for the letters. In other words, the meaning of a passage is understood by applying normal rules of grammar, syntax, context, and conventional speech.

Language is predictable. Every day we recognize and use identifiable patterns and characteristics to interpret the newspapers, books, and letters we read and every form of oral communication we hear. Words are subject to the laws that govern language.

For example, we do not normally read English words from right to left or diagonally across the page, nor do nouns become verbs and pronouns become adjectives. History does not convert to parable and narrative prose does not mysteriously become allegory. We assume an ordinary and conventional meaning for every word in the text. We seek no hidden meanings; we do not assign arbitrary meanings to words but understand them in an ordinary way. Human language is useful simply because it is predictable and kept that way by rules of grammar. It is these rules that apply to our interpretation of Scripture.

The structure of the Bible is no different from the language of any human document. The inspired authors used verbs, nouns, and prepositions following the normal laws of grammar and syntax that most of us learned in elementary school, and the language of those authors has been preserved virtually intact in our modern translations.

This is not to say that the Bible is a merely human book. It is not. The books of the Old and New Testament were given by inspiration and are the written words of God. Thus, the Bible is a unique book, unlike any other piece of literature. This fact is pivotal to our evangelical faith. However, the Bible was given in human words in ways that do not violate the conventions of language. The reason is apparent—God wants us to be clear about who He is and how we can know Him.

The task of interpretation, then, is to understand human language and how it works. We must know the meaning of words and the exact relationship these words have to one another.

"But," I hear someone say, "if the Bible is to be interpreted simply by studying it, what about prayer? Shouldn't we seek God's assistance in understanding the Bible?" Again, my answer is, "Of course," but for a different reason than most people think.

I believe almost anyone can understand the Bible, given an application of the few basic rules we apply to normal speech. The apostle Paul did say that people without God cannot understand the things of the Spirit of God (1 Cor. 2:14), but he was referring not to the words of the Bible but to their *meaning*.

It's here that prayer plays a crucial role in Bible study, and it's here that the Bible is radically different from other books. Prayer cannot help us determine the difference between prose and poetry, between nouns and verbs, or between commands and general observations about life. That understanding comes from hard mental effort, not free association, intuitive flashes, or spiritual insight.

But prayer can lead us to understand the *meaning* of Scripture—the particular truth that we need for ourselves and for those we instruct. I think that's what Paul meant in 2 Timothy 2:7 when he encouraged Timothy to "reflect on what I am saying, for the Lord will give you insight into all this [Paul's teaching]." Reflection and dependence upon God open one's eyes to see what He wants that *one* to see.

Prayer is also essential to rid our minds of pride, prejudice, and pre-conceptions to which we so doggedly cling. It enables us to hear God's Word with objectivity and susceptibility, so we can understand what is being said about our own self-will and self-reliance.

Furthermore, prayer serves in some inexplicable way to convert mere knowing into knowing God and loving Him. As Jude puts it, "Build yourselves up in your most holy faith and pray in the Holy Spirit. Keep yourselves in God's love . . ." (Jude 20–21). The truth of God cannot be rationally assimilated; the process by which the word becomes flesh and touches our hearts is suprarational— accomplished through prayer. It's for that reason that Paul knelt before the Father and prayed for his friends in Ephesus that, having heard the truth (Eph. 1:1–3:18), they would "know" what cannot otherwise be known (Eph. 3:19).

UNDERSTANDING OURSELVES

Warm-up: 1 Corinthians 1:18–25

Devote yourself to the . . .
reading of Scripture (1 Tim. 4:13).

My friends are reading more books these days to understand themselves and others better. I hope they're reading with discernment.

Solomon pointed out long ago that "of making many books there is no end, and much study wearies the body" (Eccl. 12:12). The main thing, as the wise man went on to say, is to give one's self to the book that is "given by one Shepherd" (12:11).

Some say that what a man thinks is what matters, but most of his studies about himself are a mixture of truth and error. Despite Alexander Pope's aphorism, the proper study of man is not man, but rather the study of the manual that goes with man. Our knowledge of the human race and how to fix it comes from that source. There's no other way to fully understand the stuff of which we're made.

Simply stated, the problem is one of human limitation: Human reason is inadequate. No one knows everything, so there's always a boundary to everything we know. Long ago the Greek philosopher Anaxagoras concluded that "we are certain of nothing, because our intellect is too weak, our senses are too illusory, and our life is too short." If reason is our only recourse, we're led to agnosticism.

The scientific method is likewise incomplete. It works only for subjects that can be studied by observation and experience, and some aspects of reality aren't empirically discerned. Our immaterial parts—our spirituality and sexuality, for example—can't be weighed, measured, or counted. And how can anyone make judgments about ultimate meaning and purpose in life—aspects that lie beyond the scope of our instruments and our personal sensory experience?

We would be wise not to overestimate ourselves or any other human being. Scholars may be brighter than most of us, but no one is so intelligent and well schooled that he or she knows everything there is to know. Attributing universal adequacy to any merely human method of inquiry assumes that nothing is beyond our ken, that the human race, by applying its best minds and methods, can know everything there is to know. That makes us omniscient and that's absurd.

What's worse, it's idolatry.

We don't have the where-with-all to know everything about ourselves, but when we think we do, we put too much confidence in ourselves, an overconfidence that makes us do very foolish things. We need information from outside.

Here's how Paul describes another way to *know*: "We [apostles] speak of God's secret wisdom, a wisdom that has been hidden and that God destined for our glory before time began. None of the rulers of this age understood it, for if they had, they would not have crucified the Lord of glory. However, as it is written: 'No eye has seen, no ear has heard, no mind has conceived what God has prepared for those who love him'—but God has revealed it to us by his Spirit" (1 Cor. 2:7–10a).

There is, according to Paul, a wisdom that cannot be scientifically known ("no eye has seen, no ear has heard"), nor can it be rationally determined ("no mind has conceived"). In fact, it can't be discovered at all; it must be *disclosed*.

Paul explains in the verses that follow that God's profoundest thoughts about people—who we are and why we're here—are revealed through His Word (2:10b–16). God's Word is God's manual for explaining man.

Those who love God receive His words gladly. They get in on His secrets! They get answers to their nagging questions, questions for which wise men and women have no satisfying answers, questions like, Who am I and why am I here? How can I deal with my dying and with death? What can I do about guilt and shame? How can I heal my hurting marriage? How can I suffer successfully? How can I live and like it?

On the other hand, there are those who don't love God and who won't listen to His words, whom Paul described as the "rulers of this age"—the philosophers and sages, the opinion makers and mind shapers of his time—who in their "wisdom" killed the God who came to save them, and who in the end were left to themselves with only their questions, their theories, and their fads.

And so, it seems that truly wise women and men live by the Book. They read other books, of course, but they read them all in light of the Book. As R.A. Torrey observed, "The wise man is he who believes the *Bible* against the opinions of any man. If the *Bible* says one thing, and any body of men says another, he will decide, 'This book is the Word of Him who cannot lie' " (emphasis added).

And so, if we want to understand humankind, we must read well the manual that came with him; we must "devote [ourselves] to the . . . reading of Scripture."

It's important that we do so, for, if we do not read that book, our ministries will surely fail.

MY SIN

Warm-up: Romans 7:14–8:4

*I know that nothing good lives
in me (Rom. 7:18).*

Most Christians are armed and ready to defend the depravity of man. It's a matter of creed that in one way or another, small or great, hidden or revealed, we're sinful in our origins and in all of our parts.

Yet we're inclined to think of ourselves as something of an exception, leaning more toward righteousness. What we say even on our knees about our sin is mostly theology. We've not yet discovered the depths of our depravity, and the evil of which we're capable.

So God concedes to our sin and lets us duplicate Adam's Fall, and our hearts show us the way of sin. Then we know the dark stuff of which we're made.

In our crises we see what God's eyes have seen all along: That much of us, as Gabriel Marcel said, is still unevangelized. There are those hidden scarlet sins—appalling obsessions that we love and hate, which we would never admit to anyone but ourselves. And there are those "lesser flaws" of indifference, smugness, and insensitivity, sins more gray than scarlet, which in the end can become the most serious sins of all.

Nothing can be corrected until it is exposed. So God waits patiently until our day comes, and we succumb to sudden temptations and our sins find us out. Then we know that "nothing good lives in [us]" (Rom. 7:18).

When our seams have been opened, when our unconverted parts have been disclosed, when our "strength fails because of [our] iniquity" (Ps. 31:10 NKJV), God reminds us of His cross, His forgiveness, and His incomparable grace and begins to make us new. When we fall, we fall into God's hands.

He doesn't despise our sin; He uses it. He discerns the possibilities even in our defilement, unmakes the mistakes and sets out to make us better than we've ever been before. As one of George MacDonald's characters said, "When a man or woman repents an' humbles himsel', there [God] is to lift them up—an' higher than they ever stood afore!"

Therefore, rather than mourn our humiliation we should confess it, dismiss it, and move on. We can learn to fail well—fall *forward*, as someone has said. Sin may set us back for a while, temporarily destroy our credibility, and make it necessary for us to earn once more the right to be heard.

Yet sin, repented of, can only work for good. It awakens our need for God's grace, softening us and making us more susceptible to His shaping. And it makes us much more tender with others. We can deal gently with the weak and erring—not bearing down on them—because we too are beset with sin.

John Newton knew this truth and penned these words of affirmation.

I asked the Lord that I may grow
   In faith and love and every grace.

Might more of His salvation know,
    And seek more earnestly His face.

'Twas He who taught me thus to pray,
    And He I trust has answered prayer,
But it has been in such a way
    As almost drove me to despair.

I thought that in some favored hour,
    At once He'd answer my request,
And by His love's transforming power,
    Subdue my sins and give me rest.

Instead of that He made me feel
    The hidden evils of my heart,
And bade the angry powers of hell
    Assault my soul in every part.

Nay, more, with His hand He seemed
    Intent to aggravate my woe,
Crossed all the fair designs I schemed,
    Blasted my gourds, and laid me low.

"Lord, why this?" I trembling cried.
    "Wilt Thou pursue this worm to death?"
"This is the way," the Lord replied,
    "I answer prayer for grace and faith."

A Burden Shared

"These inward trials I employ
   From sin and self to set thee free,
And cross thy schemes of earthly joy
   That thou might find thy all in Me."

THE PROBLEM WITH PREJUDICE

Warm-up: 1 Corinthians 4:1–5

Judge nothing before the appointed time;
wait till the Lord comes (1 Cor. 4:5a).

It's safe to assume that you're having difficulty with some other human being in the world, someone at work or at play, someone you employ or who employs you, someone who shares your house or whose house you share, someone you minister with or minister to. Someone is making life harder than it needs to be. It's inevitable: Simple people come and go; difficult people accumulate.

But those who make life difficult for us may not actually be guilty of wrong-doing. Sometimes we just don't understand what's going on.

Years ago I heard a story about a young salesman who worked for a company whose president made it his practice to give away turkeys to his employees for Christmas. The salesman was a bachelor who didn't know how to bake a turkey and didn't care to learn. So the gift was only a complication as far as he was concerned. Every year he had to figure out how to get rid of it.

On the day the turkeys arrived, a couple of his friends purloined the bird that was tagged with his name and substituted a dummy made of paper-mâché. The only original turkey parts were the neck and tail protruding from either end of a brown paper wrapper. The bogus bird was then presented with due formality. Our man, with turkey tucked under his arm, caught the bus for home.

As it happened, he seated himself next to a man whose melancholy was obvious and contagious. Feeling compassion for him, the salesman began a conversation in which the other's bitter circumstances began to unfold—he lost his job and had no money for Christmas. He had only a couple of dollars with which he planned to purchase a few groceries for Christmas dinner, but his funds were insufficient to buy anything but bare essentials.

The man with the bird sized up the situation and realized he had the solution to both of their problems: He could unload the turkey in a way that would be mutually beneficial. His first thought was to give it away; his second was to sell it for a few dollars, realizing that the man could salvage some of his dignity by paying for the meal.

And so he proposed the sale, explaining his dilemma and its possible resolution. The other man was elated, the exchange was made, and the bird was taken home to wife and children. They must have all gathered excitedly around the table while the turkey was unwrapped, only to discover that the bird their father had bought was a fraud.

You can imagine their disappointment and indignation. The well-meaning turkey vender, on the other hand, went home satisfied; he had done his good turn for the day.

I'm told that when he returned to work after the holidays and learned what his associates had done, he devoted most of his free time for the next month trying to track down the victim of his unintentional scam so he could set things right. He would have done anything to undo his wrong, but he never saw the man again.

That deprived family must believe to this day that they were the victims of fraud—a classic case of man's inhumanity to man. But they would be wrong; no evil was intended. The motives of the man who fobbed off the turkey were wholly good.

This story reminds me of something the apostle Paul wrote: "Judge *nothing* before the appointed time; wait till the Lord comes. He will bring to light what is hidden in darkness and will expose the motives of men's hearts. At that time each will receive his praise from God" (1 Cor. 4:4–5, emphasis added).

We can *never* judge another's intentions. We may sometimes judge their actions—human justice is rooted in that practice—but the motives of the heart are beyond our ken.

It's good to ask those who wrong us, "Can you tell me why you did what you did?" We may be surprised at what we learn. It may help us to understand, or at least be more understanding.

But even if we ask, we cannot fully appreciate another's reasons. They may not know themselves. Motives are elusive; "The heart is deceitful above all things . . . ," as Jeremiah observed, "Who can understand it?" (17:9).

And so we should not judge another's heart. Any condemnation on our part is *presumptuous:* Only God can know what another intends. And it's *premature*: We must wait until He comes. He will then "bring to light what is hidden in darkness and will expose the motives of men's hearts."

THE ELECTRONIC CHURCH

Warm-up: Hebrews 10:19–25

Let us not give up meeting together,
as some are in the habit of doing,
but let us encourage one another . . .
(Heb. 10:25).

Social scientists are telling us that television has abetted a trend toward inattentiveness. Our attention spans have been shortened by thirty-second commercials; our sense of reality has been abridged by thirty-minute episodes. I can't help wondering, therefore, what the Christian media is doing to us.

I appreciate Christian radio and television for all the good it can do—the ease with which large numbers of unchurched and untaught people can be reached, and the opportunity that shut-ins have to hear the Word. Furthermore, responsible Christian programs are a necessary adjunct to local ministries, adding another voice to the gospel and confirming its truth. It's always with two or three witnesses that a matter is established.

But I can't help wondering how many people are prevented from venturing into the real world by only participating in the electronic church.

For one thing, some people are completely dependent on the medium: They're religiously programmed from morning to night. Their days and nights are filled with endless evangelical Nirvana. They seldom venture out into the world of real people and things. It's hard for me to see any difference between this addiction and an addiction to TV soaps. Such preoccupation can't help but erode the line between fact and fantasy.

I'm also concerned about the Madison Avenue mimicry in some of those shows. Some are just so much show biz. Why can't we be more original and creative? Why must we slavishly copy secular society? What does Jerusalem have to do with Athens?

I'm dismayed too when I read of the enormous amounts of money spent to air some of these lavish programs. The cost is staggering, creating perpetual crises for the producers, and, in turn, providing "unprecedented opportunities" for viewers to send money. It reminds me too much of the advertising world and their penchant for creating needs so they can get my money. It strikes me that one's commitment to the electronic church may well remove any responsibility for local ministries and for thoughtful inquiry and careful stewardship in money matters.

Another area of concern centers on the amount of exposure and emphasis given to the stars of the more irresponsible shows. Clearly they have become gurus for many who hang on to every word and uncritically follow every suggestion. Is this not a violation of Jesus' plain warning against following one person exclusively (Matt. 23:8)? And may this not relieve us of the hard task of discovering for ourselves what the Bible says?

But my strongest objection to the so-called electronic church is simply that it isn't a church at all. It's a private affair enjoyed for one's personal benefit, and, as we know, God makes no private salvation deals.

Personal, yes; private, no. It's "with all the saints" that we grow up in all the dimensions of the love of God (Eph. 3:18).

We can't make it alone; we were made for one another. Associating with other believers is not an option for certain Christians who happen to be more gregarious than others. It's an essential part of being in God's family. It's a necessary corollary of being the children of God.

It's significant to me that while there are more Christians today than ever before, church attendance is generally down across the country. I can't help but wonder how many of the born again are merely worshiping at home.

I can't say that I blame them: I too find my brothers and sisters bothersome at times. Being in the family of faith doesn't automatically mean that we're all one happy family.

All Christians are sometimes hard to live with, myself included. Some of us are rather cranky and others are downright dull. Certainly it's easier to worship in the comfort and ease of one's home, mate at one's side, coffee cup in hand, far from the maddening crowd.

Furthermore, some church gatherings don't amount to much. As Tom Sawyer remarked, "The church ain't shucks to the circus!" Nevertheless, the church assembled is our family and we must learn to live with and love this awkward bunch. We must not "give up meeting together, as some are in the habit of doing." We should rather gather with the saints—to encourage them and to be encouraged.

ROW, ROW, ROW YOUR BOAT

Warm-up: 1 Corinthians 3:1–4:5

Men ought to regard us as servants
of Christ and as those entrusted
with the secret things of God. Now
it is required that those who have
been given a trust must prove
faithful (1 Cor. 4:1).

I recall a Far Side cartoon depicting a group of shackled slaves, standing on a pier, waiting for a Roman galley that was pulling into port. "That's a great ship," one observed, "I wonder what makes it go?"

Gary Larson's sketch reminded me of something Paul wrote long ago: "Let a man regard us as servants [under-rowers] of Christ, and stewards of the mysteries of God. In this case, moreover, it is required of stewards that one be found faithful" (1 Cor. 4:1 NASB).

Here Paul defines his two-fold task and, by extrapolation, the task of all of us who serve the church. This is ministry, stripped to its bare essentials: We are *servants* of Christ and *stewards* of the secrets of God.

The word Paul uses for "servants" is not his usual term. Literally, the word means "under-rowers," and originally referred to the slaves who pulled the sweeps in ancient, seagoing vessels. It was slave labor that kept the galleys going.

If I follow Paul's analogy, he's saying that we leaders who make the galley go, so to speak, are mere under-rowers. We're just part of the crew, seated down below decks in the lower seats, pulling on our own oar with all the other folks.

We're not up on top; that's the Captain's place. We set neither the course nor the cadence. It's His task to determine the heading and call the stroke.

This is something quite different from the usual picture of the pastor on the poop deck, resplendent in full regalia, with telescope in one hand and tiller in the other, the only one who knows where the church is going, with everyone else down below.

No, the apostle wanted to be regarded in a much different way—as one of God's galley slaves, down in the hold with the rest of God's people, pulling on an oar like everyone else.

Paul's perspective should be ours: We're not the ones to call the shots and control the ship. That's the Captain's job. The direction a church goes, the speed with which it develops, and the size to which it grows are His prerogatives. Our job is to fix our eyes on Christ and row.

Furthermore, as Paul says, we are "stewards of the mysteries of God." A steward in Paul's day was simply a butler whose job it was to rummage around in the pantry and bring out bread and wine for family meals. And thus, Paul, like a good Roman steward day after day descended into his pantry—God Himself—and brought out the good things of God's Word on which others could feed.

That's our task as well—hiding ourselves in God and in His Word, learning His secrets so we can impart them to others. As George MacDonald said, "There is that chamber—a chamber in God himself—which none can enter but the one, the individual, the peculiar man. Out of which chamber that man has to bring revelation and strength for his brethren. This is that for which he was made—to reveal the secret things of the Father" (*Unspoken Sermons*).

That's how others ought to regard us and how we ought to regard ourselves—"as servants [under-rowers] of Christ, and stewards of the mysteries of God." Those are our tasks.

And, as Paul says, it's required that "one be found faithful" on the job. We may never be prominent or particularly proficient. We may even fail. It's not necessary to succeed in order to persevere.

Faithfulness suggests a dogged refusal to fold in the face of criticism, boredom, or difficulty. Every good endeavor gets hard, usually at the point where our dreams give way to actual doing. That's when we want to lay down our oars and jump ship. But that's when we must be found in our places, patiently waiting on our Lord and serving His people.

So row, row, row your boat. We're in for the long haul, you know.

HELPING WORKERS GROW

Warm-up: Hebrews 13:7–17

*Obey your leaders and submit to
their authority. They keep watch
over you as men who must give
an account (Heb. 13:17).*

I have a friend who ranches nearby. He's involved in a small, rural church in his community. He's a church-grower of the most dedicated variety and a man of almost absolute tolerance.

He tells me they have a new pastor in their church, fresh out of seminary. The way he tells it, the school sent them a "do-it-yourself preacher kit," and now they have to put him together. I like the way he thinks. Would that all young pastors and workers had someone who loved them enough to help them get themselves together. Some folks just try to take them apart.

Whoever wrote Hebrews encouraged us to go along with those who lead us, because "they keep watch over [us] as men who must give an account" (Heb. 13:17).

Pastors have an awesome task: They watch over our immortal souls. They are, as C. S. Lewis said, "Those particular people within the whole church who have been set aside to look after what concerns us as creatures who are going to live forever."

Furthermore, they must some day stand before God and "give an account." They're not, of course, responsible for the choices we make, but they are accountable for their decisions and specifically for their willingness to speak the Word that nurtures our souls.

Assuming that our shepherds are imparting God's Word, even though ineptly, we ought to encourage them along and "obey" them, a word that suggests a yielding spirit—the exact opposite of resistance. In other words, we ought to get off their backs and get on their team.

We ought to go along with them, even if they're young. Despite our cultural focus on youth these days, most of us older folks disdain it. But as Paul wrote with regard to youthful Timothy, "If [he] comes see to it that he has nothing to fear while he is with you, for he is carrying on the work of the Lord, just as I am. No one, then, should refuse to accept him. Send him on his way in peace" (1 Cor. 16:10). In other words, we shouldn't hassle young men and women who are carrying on the work of the Lord. Rather we should lend them a hand.

We can befriend and love them. Leadership tends to isolate; leaders get lonely. They're treated differently than other folks, expected to be more nearly perfect. They're put on pedestals and stranded up there. Yet they're mere mortals with profoundly human needs, who mainly want someone to care for them and for their families, someone who will love them enough to stay on their team no matter what they do.

If they're not doing well at their job, it's never good to talk about them to others. That's serious sin (Prov. 6:16–19). We should rather talk to them, which is the biblical thing to do (Gal. 6:1–5). When we've loved them long and have won the right to be heard, we can "gently instruct, in the hope that God will . . . [lead] them to a knowledge of the truth" (2 Tim. 2:25). We all need gentle criticism; as the proverb says, "Pleasant words promote instruction" (Prov 16:21).

Hopefully, they'll listen. If leaders aren't willing to be checked and balanced they shouldn't be leading. "He who cannot obey, cannot lead," as Benjamin Franklin once said.

We should pray for those who lead us. An inspired apostle urged us to pray for all who are in authority; that's the biblical thing to do (1 Tim. 2:1–2). Only God can change another. If we try too hard to modify others, it puts an intolerable strain on the relationship. But God can change anyone. Entrust people to God. Prayer (the highest expression of our dependence on Him) moves men as well as mountains.

And we should pray with them. We can drop by or call in to ask about personal and ministry needs and spend a moment or two in intercessory prayer. It doesn't take much of our time, but it can pay off handsomely. There's no better way to encourage another than to place the demands of ministry upon God.

And finally, while we're concerned with the care and feeding of workers, I should point out that the same one who said to *pray* for laborers (Luke 10:2), also said to *pay* them—"The worker deserves his wages" (Luke 10:7).

We should show them *double* honor (1 Tim. 5:17), and pay them more than respect. We don't have to keep God's servants impoverished to keep them poor in spirit.

Paul reflected on two occasions that the practice of underpaying one's workers is inhumane—like the niggardly practice of muzzling an ox so that it cannot graze while it works (1 Tim. 5:18; 1 Cor. 9:9).

Furthermore, he reminded the Galatian church that "anyone who receives instruction in the word must share all good [material] things with his instructor." We should do so because "God cannot be mocked. A man reaps what he sows. The one who sows to please his sinful nature, from that nature will reap destruction; the one who sows to please the Spirit, from the Spirit will reap eternal life" (Gal. 6:6–8).

Paying one's leaders and workers adequately is what Paul calls sowing to "please the Spirit." To not pay them well is to "sow to [the] sinful nature" and manifests a miserly spirit, which in turn produces death and destruction in the parish. The cost of such economy is too great a price to pay.

In summary, it seems to me that the issue is investment and that the bottom line is profit to the Body of Christ. We should go along with our leaders and fully support them in their task, "so that their work will be a joy, not a burden, for that would be of no advantage to you" (Heb. 13:17).

Our refusal to help with the training of good shepherds becomes irrational in the light of these words. Melancholy, beleaguered leaders are a wasting asset. It's a disadvantage to dishonor them. We should rather "respect those who work hard among [us], who are over [us] in the Lord and who admonish [us]. [And] hold them in the highest regard in love because of their work" (1 Thess. 5:12).

What's needed, then, is someone who will minister to those who minister to us, who will pay attention to their hidden hurts and who will help them stay faithful to their task through loving censure and support.

THE IMPOSSIBLE DREAM

Warm-up: Genesis 18:1–15

Is anything too hard for the LORD?
(Gen. 18:14).

"Is anything too hard for the LORD?" That's what the stranger asked Abraham and Sarah when he met them under the oaks at Mamre. It was a question that became a maxim in Israel.

Jeremiah had the same question when he bought a piece of ground near Jerusalem. The Babylonians were outside the city; the siege was on. They were not likely to give it up or go away.

Yet Jeremiah's purchase was made in good faith because God had promised to give the land back to Judah one day. So, based on that word, Jeremiah signed the deed. When challenged he asked, Is anything too hard for the Lord? (Jer. 32:17, 27).

When the stranger first posed the question to Abraham and Sarah, they were waiting for God to come through. Twenty-five years before, God had promised them a son. Now Abraham, almost one hundred years old, was "as good as dead" (Heb. 11:12). Sarah herself was almost ninety, and "it ceased to be with Sarah after the manner of women" (Gen. 18:11 KJV).

Nevertheless, the stranger persisted, saying, "I will return to you at the appointed time next year and Sarah will have a son" (Gen. 18:14). Sarah laughed, but one year later "the LORD did for Sarah what he had promised. Sarah became pregnant and bore a son to Abraham in his old age, at the very time God had promised him" (Gen. 21:1–2).

It was an impossible task that God had—making life in Sarah's dead body and bringing salvation into the world. But the stranger was right: "Is anything too hard for the LORD?"

There are those impossible people with whom we work who seem to have no heart for God, who are out of touch with reality and utterly untouched by the preaching of God's Word.

There are those impossible boards that are encumbered by men and women who have consecrated themselves to mild discipleship and devotion and who think and act as though God had never spoken.

There are those impossible communities where everything ugly and obscene is permitted and cultivated, but no one wants us to talk about the loveliness of Jesus.

There are those impossible churches with their unofficial power centers and self-appointed aristocracies who seem bent upon frustrating every God-given plan.

And then, there's you and me. It's an impossible job God has—ridding us of our private perversions, our bad habits and compulsions, the unholy attitudes and actions that plague us and inhibit us and, despite God's extraordinary grace, make us feel defiled and unqualified to serve.

Yes, there are people, places, and things that are impossible, but "What is impossible with men is possible with God" (Luke 18:27). He has His way of doing what cannot otherwise be done. He will not be hurried, but

He's always at hand. He "is able to do immeasurably more than all we ask or imagine, according to his power that is at work within us" (Eph. 3:20).

As Hudson Taylor learned, "There are three stages in every great work of God. First it is impossible. Then it is difficult. And then it is done!"

WISING UP

Warm-up: Proverbs 4:1–27

Though it cost all you have,
get understanding (Prov. 4:7).

Some of my friends are going off to Bible school or seminary to pick up a theological degree. They tell me they need something more. I know the feeling. I took off once myself.

Schooling is a good thing, but I don't know why anyone would *unnecessarily* burden himself with that yoke. Study—even Bible study—is a grind that's hard on us and hard on our families. It's never what it's cracked up to be. We ought to have a very good reason for going.

Some of us matriculate because of a deep dissatisfaction within. We feel undervalued and believe that more theological education will give us the lift that we need.

But that illusion fades with time and though one can acquire useful knowledge on almost any campus, the actual learning process often leaves us more empty and defeated than we've ever been before. Personally I don't know any recent graduates who necessarily feel better about themselves simply because they've finished the course and know a little more than most of their fellows.

It's easy to get caught up in a system that gives good marks for good works. Satisfaction, which is often deferred in the off-campus world, comes almost immediately in the classroom. But though scholarship and achievement may enchant us for a while, the glory soon fades. No one can retain the prizes of academic distinction very long.

Furthermore, knowledge—even knowledge of God—doesn't necessarily lead us to know God. It can, in fact, make us more prideful and push us away from Him. "Knowledge puffs up," as Paul says (1 Cor. 8:1). It doesn't necessarily build us up. We can chatter on about God and talk as though we know Him, when in fact we do not know Him at all. Sometimes I think that the greatest deterrent to knowing God is knowing too much about Him.

I think that's why there's so much melancholy on campus—even on Bible school campuses. Chasing after knowledge as a thing in itself, as the wise man said, is chasing after the wind. "For with much wisdom comes much sorrow; the more knowledge, the more grief" (Eccl. 1:18).

Please understand that I have deep empathy for truth and for education, especially for biblical studies. The God who endowed us with reason and intellect intended us to use these faculties. Without attention to hard thinking we degenerate into idiosyncrasies and even heresy. (As a friend of mine says, you can always tell when people stop thinking—at about age forty their heads go soft and they become sentimental or else their heads get hard and they become impossible—an aging process he describes as a "hardening of the categories.")

But having mere facts in our heads doesn't make us better men and women. Schooling feeds our minds but not necessarily our hearts, and it's what's in our hearts that determines the fruit we bear for God. There's more to life than being skilled and learned. We make our mark on the world by character and wisdom.

Thinking of going back to school should force us to know why we're going. We may pick up useful exegetical and biblical knowledge there and that may be just what we need. Everyone needs additional tools in the tool box and more skill at using them. But no college, university, seminary, or Bible school can make us more godly, nor can they endow us with wisdom and common sense. We can be knowledgeable with other people's knowledge, but no human being can make us wise. The disciplines of character and wisdom are the products of God's grace, taught to us through the instruction of the Word and in the school of hard knocks.

And we can get that education at home.

REALISTIC EXPECTATIONS

Some fell along the path. . . .
Some fell on rocky places. . . .
Other seed fell among thorns. . . .
Still other seed fell on good soil. . .
(Matt. 13:4–8).

The wisest observers of life have remarked that if you wish to love people you shouldn't expect too much of them. There's a wealth of reality and humanity in that observation.

Jesus, who was the ultimate realist in such matters, prepared His disciples for this uncommon idea by telling them a story about a farmer who went out to sow. As the sower was scattering the seed, some fell on the hard path and the birds ate it up. Other seed fell where there wasn't much soil. The seed germinated and sprang up quickly, but the sun soon beat it down and the plants withered because they had no root. Other seed fell among thorns, which grew up and choked the plants. Still other seed fell on good soil, where it produced a bumper crop—"a hundred, sixty or thirty times what was sown" (Matt. 13:3–8).

And then Jesus explained (13:18–23). He said that the seed is "the message about the kingdom"—that good news about the coming of the long expected King.

He said that some wouldn't receive that announcement at all. They're unwilling to be edified; the seed never penetrates the hard surface of their hearts, and so the evil one comes and snatches it away before it can begin to grow. The hard hearted have no memory of ever having heard.

Other seed will fall on hearts that though initially receptive, will eventually prove resistant. Beneath the apparent yielding there is no compliance, and when the hard times come, the seed shrivels and dies.

Still other seed will be sown among thorns, which will grow up and choke the plant. These are those who also receive the seed with apparent delight, but who are weedy, transient, and limited in heart, and in the end, their preoccupation with their careers, the pursuit of more money, and the other vexations of life overwhelm the Word and they have no more time for the truth.

But still other seed will fall on good soil and prove fruitful, "a hundred, sixty or thirty times what was sown"—a prize-winning crop of goodness and likeness to Christ, produced by the life inherent in the seed.

The point of the parable is very clear: Receptivity is the business of the individual human being in whom the seed is sown. Each one must *choose* to hear. As Jesus said, "He who has ears, let him hear" (13:9).

The extent to which an individual wants to understand the Word of the kingdom determines the amount of the Word that is heard. "Whoever has will be given more, and he will have an abundance" (13:12). Those who want to know more, get more. The wise get wiser (Prov. 4:5–7).

But those who decide not to understand the Word will be left with less of it than they had. "Whoever does not have, even what he has will be taken from him" (13:12). Truth becomes less and less appealing and convincing to them and they inevitably wander away into illusions and lies. As Paul put it, when people refuse to love the truth they'll believe anything (2 Thess. 2:11; cf. 2 Chron. 18:1–27).

In some instances, life is just that simple: What you want is what you get, and a little bit more.

I take it, then, that our business as sowers is merely to sow—widely, almost indiscriminately, here, there, everywhere, "admonishing and teaching *everyone* with all wisdom, so that we may present everyone perfect in Christ" (Col. 1:28, emphasis added).

When received, the seed will do its work. Those who hear it will want to hear more and the seed will begin to grow, unobtrusively, invisibly generating the crop that is seen.

But inevitably, there will be those who, despite our prayerful earnestness and our faithful sowing, will be unproductive. In fact, people will be left worse off than they were before we met them—less human and alive than they ever were before (cf. 2 Cor. 2:15–16).

If so, please know that it's not our fault. We've given the Word, the seed has been sown, and that's all we'll ever be able to do. There were some on whom even Jesus could do no mighty works (cf. Matt. 13:58).

And so it comes to this: If we really think we're going to save everyone we're being very naive. Some days, no matter how hard we try, we'll leave the world a worse place than we found it. Count on it.

THE CURE FOR CONFLICT

Warm-up: James 4:1–10

*What causes fights and quarrels
among you? Don't they come from
your desires that battle within you?
(James 4:1)*

Conflict, like death and taxes, is unavoidable. Nations rage, neighbors feud, siblings strive, lovers quarrel, and churches fight. One zigs, the other zags. Life is full of dissonance. What can we do?

One sure way to temporarily conciliate another is to lose—give in. And some would argue that humility and submission demand it. But God-fearing men and women aren't meant to be push-overs. They seek first the kingdom of God and His righteousness and not peace at any cost. "The wisdom that comes from heaven is *first of all* pure; then peace-loving" (James 3:17, emphasis added).

Furthermore, no one wins when one party always wins. Winning under those conditions is a wasted, Pyrrhic victory.

Antagonists can dig in and defend rigid (or shifting) positions and try to wear one another down by argument and contest of will, or one can pull rank and insist on surrender, but no one gets to agreement either way. As Samuel Butler said, "he that complies against his will is of the same opinion still."

When all else fails we can beat up on one another—verbally if not physically—like the lawyers who, when they found themselves on the short end of a debate with Jesus, resorted to name-calling. ("We be not born of fornication," they cackled, clearly implying that He was [John 8:41 NKJV].)

Or we can do it James' peaceable way. Consider his counsel: "What causes fights and quarrels among you? Don't they come from your desires that battle within you? You want something but don't get it. You kill and covet, but you cannot have what you want. You quarrel and fight. You do not have, because you do not ask God. When you do ask, you do not receive, because you ask with wrong motives, that you may spend what you get on your pleasures" (James 4:1–3).

"What causes fights and quarrels?" Good question. James gets to the root of the problem. Conflict comes from our "desires," a word suggesting "something that satisfies." Underlying all conflict is this hidden factor—one's personal interest and longing for satisfaction.

People are bundles of needs, wants, hopes, dreams, fears, and ambitions that are doing battle within them, fighting for satisfaction. It's these cross-currents of personal concern that put us on the road to conflict with others. When the pursuit of our own interests is blocked by others' pursuits of their own interests we become frustrated and conflict develops. (Consider, for example, what happens when Young Husband comes home seeking silence and solitude and encounters Young Wife, whose most intelligent conversation all day long has been with a two-year old child!)

This is why arguments are almost never about the

subject under debate. Underneath the conflict is the covert factor of personal concern. These concerns are the interests that motivate people; they are the silent movers behind the positions we take.

Therefore, the first step in conflict resolution is to temporarily set aside the surface problems and the positions we've adopted and try to get in touch with one another's underlying concerns. As Paul said, "Each of you should look not only to your own interests, but also to the interests of others" (Phil. 2:4–5).

That takes a bit of doing. We have to peel away the outer layers of perceptions and emotions until we get to the heart. Ultimately, the resolution of any conflict lies not in the conflict itself but in people's hearts.

And that means loving one another—putting ourselves in the other's shoes; trying to see the merits of their case. It means forgoing blame, not holding them responsible for the problem. It means sending "I" messages rather than "you" messages—talking about ourselves and how we feel rather than what the other has done. It means "believing all things," rather than putting the worst interpretation on what the other side says or does. It means refusing to pout or stonewall or walk out. It means apologizing when we get out of hand.

It means asking questions and listening actively and acknowledging what's being said, asking the other party to spell out carefully and clearly exactly what is meant, requesting that ideas be repeated if there is ambiguity or uncertainty, and repeating what we have heard the other person say, all of which can lead to understanding.

Once we understand one another's bottom-line concerns we can begin to invent options for mutual gain, collaborating in a hard-headed, side by side search for solutions that will benefit both.

But, you ask, what if the other party won't dance and we're denied and left wanting (James 4:2)? For some that's an invitation to "quarrel and fight," and even to "kill." (Most killings are not premeditated but rather crimes of passion, deeply regretted after the fact.)

James has an unexpected answer: We should ask God to meet our needs *His* way (4:2–3). Rather than take matters into our own hands, it's far better to ask God to supply what we must have, and to ask with sincerity— "Not my will but yours be done."

It does no good to blame others or brood over our plight. Rather we should talk to the one who knows our deepest needs long before we become aware of them and who cares about us more than we can imagine. We can tell Him about our anger and hurt, our fears and frustration; He can handle any emotion. But we should then ask Him to meet our needs His way, for, as James would say, we should not ask "with wrong motives."

But when God meets our needs, "he gives us *more* grace" (4:6, emphasis added). Frustrated desire becomes an open door to more of God and an opportunity to have more of our needs met than we could ever imagine.

To satisfy our interests apart from God is a serious matter! Follow James' argument: "You adulterous people, don't you know that friendship with the world is hatred toward God? Anyone who chooses to be a friend of the world becomes an enemy of God. Or do you think Scripture says without reason that the spirit he caused to live in us envies intensely? But he gives us more grace? That is why Scripture says: 'God opposes the proud but gives grace to the humble' " (4:4–6).

God is like a jealous husband who longs to satisfy the deepest desires of his bride. All she has to do is ask. Perhaps He will give the very thing desired or He may, out of infinite wisdom, substitute another, better thing, but His solutions are always the best solutions of all.

But when we fail to ask and insist on satisfying ourselves in ways other than His, we are like a wanton, adulterous wife who will not come to her mate with her needs. Or, to pick up on James' mixed metaphor, we've made friends with the world, since self-assertion, and not simple dependence on God, is the secular way of satisfying one's needs.

Since, therefore, we belong to a loving, caring Lord, we should "submit . . . to God [since our circumstances are His will]. Resist the devil, and he will flee from you. [Though he would entice us to fight for self-interest at the expense of another, he has no defense against faith]. Come near to God and he will come near to you. [He responds lovingly and patiently to our needs]. Wash your hands, you sinners, and purify your hearts, you double-minded. Grieve, mourn and wail. [To insist upon our interests is a serious sin for it produces "disorder and every evil practice" (3:16)]. Change your laughter to mourning and your joy to gloom. [Self-assertion is no laughing matter!] Humble yourselves before the Lord, and he will lift you up [an unequivocal promise!]" (4:7–10)

Coming to a Father who delights in us and who gives us dignity is the added dimension that books on conflict-resolution seem to miss. Perhaps their authors do not know God and do not know that He longs to give His children more than they could ever get on their own.

WISDOM FROM ABOVE

Warm-up: James 3:13–18

*Who is wise and understanding
among you? (James 3:13).*

"Who is wise and understanding among you?" James asks. That's a good question, especially for those who teach.

Wisdom isn't what we think it is. Robert Fulghum was very close to the truth when he concluded that "wisdom is not at the top of graduate school mountain, but there in the sandbox at nursery school," where we learn the important things in life: "Share everything. Play fair. Don't hit. Put things back. Clean up your own messes. Don't take what isn't yours. Say you're sorry when you hurt someone. . . . Everything you need to know is in there somewhere: The Golden Rule, and love . . . and sane living" (*All I Ever Really Needed to Know I Learned in Kindergarten*).

Wisdom is not so much a matter of *knowing* as *being*. James says, "Let him [who is wise] show it by his *good life*, by deeds done in the humility that comes from wisdom" (3:13, emphasis added). Wisdom is the "good life." It is the fleshing out of morality, values, character.

Wisdom is first *pure*, that is, morally clean— characterized by integrity, candor, and honesty (3:17). It does not compromise or cut corners.

It is also *peace-loving*. Passively it is tranquil and peaceable rather than quarrelsome. Actively it makes and maintains peace.

It is *considerate*, a word whose Greek root is used for old wine. Wisdom is not harsh and acerbic, but mellow and sweet, easy to be around and easy to work with.

It is *submissive*, or, as the King James Version translates it, "easy to be intreated." It is flexible without being uncertain; convinced without being rigid.

It is *full of mercy*. Wisdom is tenderhearted without being soft. It empathizes with the limitations and failures of others and handles the most fragile and intensely personal things with sensitivity and compassion.

It is *impartial*. It does not divide or discriminate. It is not racist, sexist, or elitist. It seeks the lost and the little ones and sits with them.

It is *sincere*—not hypocritical. It aims to do what it knows to do and admits to what it cannot yet do.

Workers who are wise in these ways are never irrelevant, nor can they be ignored. Though often nameless, they are never useless. They have lasting influence on others; they multiply themselves manifold, sowing seeds of well-being and wisdom, leaving behind a "harvest of righteousness" (3:18).

The indispensable quality of a good teacher is character. Education is mostly the impress of one's "good life" on others. "The most reverende [godly] person doth more affect the heart, though with common words, than an irreverent man with the most exquisite preparations" (George MacDonald).

THE TEACHER AND THE TONGUE

Warm-up: James 3:1–12

If anyone is never at fault in what
he says, he is a perfect man . . . (James 3:2).

Words, said Aristotle, are what set human beings above the lower animals. Not necessarily.

Words can bring us down: "Not many of you should presume to be teachers," writes James, "because you know that we who teach will be judged more strictly. We all stumble in many ways. If anyone is never at fault in what he says, he is a perfect man, able to keep his whole body in check" (James 3:1–2).

I'm a teacher by trade—a vendor of words. It's a good profession—one of the "greater gifts" we're encouraged to seek (1 Cor. 12:31)—yet there is peril in the task: Teachers are more culpable than others.

We're at risk because we multiply words, and as the wise man said, "When words are many, sin is not absent" (Prov. 10:19), a text which, as Augustine said, "frightens me a good deal."

James indicts all of us when he says, "If anyone is not at fault in what he says, he is a perfect [mature] man, able to keep his whole body in check." Like good physicians everywhere, Dr. James invites us to stick out our tongue because that member of our body, more than any other, reveals the state of our being.

Our tongues tell on us; we're only as good as our words.

James underscores the importance of the tongue. Small bits guide large horses; small rudders steer large ships; little things mean a lot. So it is with the tongue. Little words can mean a lot: "The tongue is a small part of the body, but it makes great boasts [boasts of great things]" (3:5).

The tongue has immense power and lasting influence. A word or two, blurted out in an unguarded moment can bring everlasting harm to another. "One proud, lordly word, one needless contention, can . . . blast the fruit of all we are doing" (Richard Baxter). Words cannot be unsaid nor the damage undone.

"The tongue also is a fire," James contends, "a world of evil among the parts of the body. It corrupts the whole person [and] sets the whole course of his life on fire" (3:6). It blazes its way through our private and public worlds like a run-away forest fire, leaving behind scorched earth, devastation, and ruin. It seeps and creeps into every nook and cranny of our bodies, permeating and polluting all that we say. It affects the entire course of our lives, from the irritability of childhood, through the sullenness of adolescence, to the crankiness and irascibility of old age.

Furthermore, our talking cannot be restrained. "All kinds of birds, reptiles and creatures of the sea are being tamed and have been tamed by man, but no man can tame the tongue. It is a restless evil, full of deadly poison" (3:7–8). Every life-form can be domesticated or constrained to serve us, but not the tongue. It cannot be commanded or controlled. James says unequivocally,

"No man can tame the tongue" (3:8). Although I "watch my ways and keep my tongue from sin" and "put a muzzle on my mouth," my heart grows "hot within me," the fire burns, and then I speak with my tongue (Ps. 39:1–3).

And there's more: "With the tongue we praise our Lord and Father, and with it we curse men, who have been made in God's likeness. Out of the same mouth come praise and cursing. My brothers, this should not be. Can both fresh water and salt water flow from the same spring? My brothers, can a fig tree bear olives, or a grapevine bear figs? Neither can a salt spring produce fresh water" (James 3:9–12).

How odd—that blessing and cursing pour from the same aperture! But therein lies the solution. If it's true that a spring emits brackish water one moment and fresh water the next, we must consider the *source*. And so it is with the tongue.

The heart is the fountainhead of every word, either corrupting it or correcting it. Jesus said, "The good man brings good things out of the good stored up in his heart, and the evil man brings evil things out the evil stored up in his heart. For out of the overflow of his heart his mouth speaks" (Luke 6:45). Apt words come from a heart that is governed by God.

The message is the heart of the messenger. Communication courses are useful and homiletics helps, but no amount of discipline and training can quell the wayward tongue.

James is right—"No *man* can tame the tongue"—but there's plenty of help from Another.

WHEAT AND TARES

Warm-up: Matthew 13:24–30, 36–43

Let both grow together until the
harvest (Matt. 13:30).

Jesus told this story about seeds.

> The kingdom of heaven is like a man who sowed good seed in his field. But while everyone was sleeping, his enemy came and sowed weeds among the wheat, and went away. When the wheat sprouted and formed heads, then the weeds also appeared. . . .
> The servants asked him, "Do you want us to go and pull them up?"
> "No," he answered, "because while you are pulling the weeds, you may root up the wheat with them. Let both grow together until the harvest. At that time I will tell the harvesters: First collect the weeds and tie them in bundles to be burned; then gather the wheat and bring it into my barn" (Matt. 13:24–30).

Jesus explained, saying, "The one who sowed the good seed is the Son of Man. The field is the world, and the good seed stands for the sons of the kingdom. The weeds are the sons of the evil one, and the enemy who sows them is the devil. The harvest is the end of the age, and the harvesters are angels" (13:37–39).

There you have it: The sons of God and the sons of the devil will co-exist until the end of the age. And *then*, "the Son of Man will send out his angels and they will weed out . . . everything that causes sin and all who do evil. . . . He who has ears, let him hear" (13:41).

There's much to be said about this parable, and much that has been said. Its interpretations are legion.

We can, on the basis of this parable, divide the world into two classes—those who are genuinely born of God and those who are genuinely bogus.

We can also conclude that the two classes are initially indistinguishable. Very often it's impossible to see any difference at all between an emerging son of God and a good old boy who belongs to the devil.

Furthermore, you can be assured that the differences will become apparent as the plants grow old. We'll know others by the perfecting of their fruit: God's men and women will get to be more and more like their Father as they age. And likewise for the devil's.

But it seems to me that among all possible applications, Jesus was surely making one: Don't be a tare-upper! There's a great danger in damning others. "Christ knoweth," John Woolman wrote, "what is in need of purging." We should rather get on with the business of helping the Son of Man sow and leave the final judgments to Him.

Certainly there are occasions when we must vigorously "contend for the faith that was once for all entrusted to the saints" (Jude 3), and "refute those who oppose it" (Titus 1:9), but we should not be preoccupied with contention. (And woe to us if we welcome it.)

How much time we've wasted and how much harm we've done because we have not ears to hear! I think of the early disciples who, with Elijah-like fury, wanted Jesus to rain down fire and brimstone on the infidels of that day, and I recall His stern rebuke (Luke 9:54). And I think of my friend nearby who has made it his life's work to hassle local heretics. I admire his passion, but I'm uneasy about his priorities.

Let them be. "Let them both grow . . . until the harvest." As Jesus' promised, "Every plant that my heavenly Father has not planted will be pulled up by the roots. Leave them . . . " (Matt. 15:13).

THE GOOD SHEPHERD

Warm-up: Ezekiel 34:1–31

*I myself will search for my sheep
and look after them (Ezek. 34:11).*

I've been a shepherd all my life. When I was younger, living down in the cedar breaks of Texas, I had a small hand of Shropshires. Now that I'm in Idaho, I have another flock.

My shepherding experience has taught me that sheep come in all varieties—there are the little ones that have to be carried, the cripples that can't keep up, the nursing ewes that won't be hurried, and the little black sheep that are always on the outside. There are the bell-wethers that always want to be out front, and the bullies that butt and push to get their own way.

There are those that graze their way into lostness, and others that deliberately flee from the shepherd.

There are those that are afraid to follow, and those that delight to be led.

All need a good shepherd.

It was Ezekiel's task to care for Israel's exiles, dispersed throughout the world. He said, "they were scattered because there was no shepherd, and when they were scattered they became food for all the wild animals. [They] wandered over all the mountains and on every high hill. They were scattered over the whole earth, and no one searched or looked for them" (34:5–6).

Their disbanding was their own fault, of course—the result of years of indifference, and then resistance, to God. They were described as those who had looked to their own idols and shed blood, had defiled their neighbors' wives, and had done "detestable things" (33:26). That's why they were now disenfranchised and scattered around the world.

Yet Ezekiel said that no matter what Israel had done they were still God's sheep, and the Good Shepherd would go looking for them (34:11). "I will search for the lost and bring back the strays," he said (34:16).

Truly good shepherds don't look down on lost sheep, it seems. They look after them. Even if the sheep aren't thinking about the shepherd at all, or even if they are and don't want him, he pursues them to the ends of the world.

Furthermore, Ezekiel said, when Israel's Good Shepherd found His sheep he looked after them: "As a shepherd looks after his scattered flock, when he is with them, so will I look after my sheep" (34:12). He scrutinized every animal for the signs of hounding and abuse, the wounds and residue of their resistance.

And then the Good Shepherd promised to do what Israel's other shepherds were unwilling to do: "I will bind up the injured and strengthen the weak" (34:16).

He had compassion on the afflicted and the handicapped, on those wounded by their own sin. He encouraged those who were weak and likely to stray; He protected them from those who would drive them away from the flock, the fold, and the goodness of the Shepherd. All that the Good Shepherd did for His own.

But, as Ezekiel says, there was more. Another Good

Shepherd was on the way. This one would be one with the Father, making tangible His pastoral compassion: "I will place over them one [unique] shepherd, my servant David, and he will tend them; he will tend them and be their shepherd. I the LORD will be their God, and my servant David will be prince among them. I the LORD have spoken (Ezek. 34:23–24).

Another Good Shepherd! Not David revisited but David's long-awaited Son, our Lord Jesus, "that great Shepherd of the sheep" (Heb. 13:20). He too saw God's wayward flock as "sheep without a shepherd," had compassion on them, and "began teaching them many things" (Mark 6:34). He, like his Father, "came to seek and to save what was lost" (Luke 19:10). The "lost" in this case, were the publicans, sinners, and scalawags who sat with Zacchaeus and befriended Jesus.

He's the one who left the "ninety-nine on the hills" and went "to look for the one that wandered off," forever establishing the value of one soul and the Father's unwillingness that "any of these little ones should be lost" (Matt. 18:12–14). His love for one vagrant was enough to send Him to earth.

His otherness, His separation from sin did not and does not cause Him to separate Himself from sinners. He doesn't distance Himself from us when we disappoint Him nor does He relinquish us when we flee. Lost sheep are not doomed. He follows us into our darkness, where, perhaps, we hoped to elude Him, and He gathers us in before we can escape. He is the Good Shepherd who lays down His life for the sheep—errant sheep (cf. John 10:1–18), or, as Paul said, "While we were still sinners, Christ died for us" (Rom. 5:8).

I have a lot to learn about shepherding. If I would be a good shepherd I must care not only for those who meekly follow but also for those who do not. Like Father and Son, I must be the friend and shepherd of sinners and gather them in—the objectionable, the obnoxious, the corrupted men and women, the bad little boys and girls. They're all the lost God sent His Son to save.

But, as old shepherds tell me, no one can learn to be a good shepherd; it's a profession that cannot be taught. One must be born to it.

If I want the knack, then, it must be born in me— conceived by the only Good Shepherd worthy of the name. Any tenderness, any caring, any love for the lost is first in His heart—then He puts it in mine.

BACK TO THE FUTURE

Warm-up: 2 Peter 3:1–15

*Since everything will be destroyed
in this way, what kind of people
ought you to be? (2 Peter 3:11).*

There's an apocalyptic mood in the air these days. A lot of folks are preoccupied with the future.

Some of it is simple curiosity. They just want to know what's in the offing. Since, as Charles Kettering said, we expect to spend the rest of our lives in the future, we want to be reasonably sure of what it's going to be.

Some of it is dread. Wars and rumors of war persist. More and more madmen are poised to blow up our earth. Some wonder if they're going to get out of the future alive. Even Christians are caught in the tide—judging from the recent spate of books and sermons on the subject.

It concerns me, though, that much of our current preoccupation with future things tends toward end-time scenarios and time tables that go beyond what we know. This is not the emphasis of Scripture.

Don't get me wrong. I enjoy theologizing as much as the next person, but we ought to distinguish between what we know for certain and what we don't. As an inspired apostle warns us, we must avoid going "beyond what is written" (1 Cor. 4:6).

Going beyond can get us into trouble. In the extreme there are those dear folks who announce the date of the Day of the Lord, only to see the day come and go. I feel for them. It would be hard to live down a gaff like that.

But even we who are more cautious and less certain can sometimes go too far. We should always remember Jesus' words: "It is not for you to know the times or dates the Father has set by his own authority" (Acts 1:7).

It concerns me that some make these small differences the tests for inclusion in the church, or at least in one's local church. It occurred to me once, as I was reading a certain group's doctrinal statement on last things, that neither Martin Luther nor John Calvin, if they were alive today, would be welcome in that body. In fact, I couldn't think of a single pre-twentieth-century Christian who would.

It would be so much better if we would love one another more, as Jesus said, and "stand firm in one spirit, contending as one man for the faith of the gospel" (Phil. 1:27), instead of quarreling among ourselves. We enervate ourselves by fighting each other instead of the enemy.

And then, I wonder what effect we're having on those outside the fold. Christian works on end-time themes are appearing now in secular book stores shelved, not with religious books, but with material on metaphysics, augury, divination, New Age, and fortune telling. It doesn't take long to figure out that others view them as just another form of the current craze to divine the future. I'm not sure they're getting the right message.

Actually we don't know much about the future, and, what's more, God doesn't seem to want us to know. He has deliberately left much unsaid and unexplained, and for a good reason: It might actually diminish our faith if we knew too much. We'd spend our time kibitzing—looking over God's shoulder to see how He's getting along—instead of getting on with our job. He wants us to trust Him and His faithfulness (not our fold-outs) from beginning to end.

According to Peter, there are only two things to remember about the future (2 Peter 3:10–12).

First of all, Peter insists, "the day of the Lord will come like a thief. The heavens will disappear with a roar; the elements will be destroyed by fire, and the earth and everything in it will be laid bare" (3:10).

Our story is not an idiot's tale. Though man is now having his day, all history is tending toward the Day of the Lord. His Day will come! One of these days He will appear, the heavens will disappear, the earth and everything in it will be burned up, and God will set about making a new heaven and new earth from the debris.

The world, like a time bomb, is ticking its way toward oblivion. God is delaying, not because He is indifferent or impotent, but because He does not want anyone to perish, "but everyone to come to repentance" (3:9). His time table is determined by His love for the world, not by its rotation nor by the number of times it circles the sun. That's why He's waiting, and waiting, and waiting.

But someday, suddenly, the future will become the present, and then everything in this earth that men and women have put their minds and their money on will immediately vanish into thin air.

That certainty may not be obvious on the face of it. It appears that our world, though it's getting very old, is rolling relentlessly on, an illusion that has led some to believe in the immutability of matter—that this universe of ours, as Carl Sagan insists, "is all that is, all that has ever been and all that will ever be" (cf. 3:3–4).

I think of non-Christian scientists, cynical unbelievers, and others who believe that matter is all that there is. Yes, but also of those of us who believe in Christ, but who also believe in our hearts that matter is all that matters—that our earthly concerns, our vacation condos, and our capital assets are the things that will endure. If so, we, like the rest of the world, will certainly suffer loss. It's all going to burn up some day.

Given the certainty of that destruction, Peter makes his second emphasis in the form of a question, "What kind of people ought you to be?" (3:11). That, and that alone, is the apocalyptic question.

Peter answers, "You ought to live holy and godly [worshipful] lives as you look forward to the day of God and speed its coming" (3:11–12). And he says again, "So then, dear friends, since you are looking forward to this [the new heaven and new earth], make every effort to be found, spotless [unspoiled by the world], blameless and at peace [untroubled] with him. Bear in mind that our Lord's patience means salvation . . ." (3:14).

Simply put, real devotion to the future is a matter of holy living today. Peter spells it out in terms of two characteristics—holiness and tranquility.

God has called us to *holiness*, a word that suggests that one acts differently than others act under the same circumstances. It suggests serious thought and presence of mind in response to adversity and opposition. It means humility, durability, magnanimity, justice, and a love for others that is as rich and inclusive as God's (cf. 2 Peter 1:1–11).

Tranquility comes from being informed—from the revelation that Someone up there is minding the store. Those who know that God holds the last moment are not uptight about the next.

Godliness and tranquility, therefore, are the marks of those whose passions are restrained by the future and who thus live differently from those who are unaware.

I like the way Evelyn Underhill puts it:

[Those who understand what God is doing] have three distinguishing characteristics—Tranquility, Gentleness and Strength, which suggests an immense depth and a steadiness that comes from the fact that our small action is part of the total action of God, whose Spirit, as another saint has said, 'works always in tranquility.' Fuss and feverishness, anxiety, intensity, intolerance, instability, pessimism, and wobble, and every kind of hurry and worry—these, even on the highest levels, are signs of the self-made and self-acting soul; the spiritual parvenu [upstart]. The saints are never like that. They share the quiet and noble qualities of the One to whom they belong.

What can I say then about some of our other efforts to win those around us who are running scared and trying to find safety in commodities that will someday self-destruct. "Turn or burn" T-shirts? Bumper stickers warning that the driver of the car on which they appear may suddenly disappear? End-of-the-world comic books designed to scare the living daylights out of small children deemed not ready for the Rapture? Can anyone be blamed for laughing?

No, if our friends are to be won at all it is not our end-time scheming but our genial, Christ-like bearing that will bring about their salvation (3:9, 15). That, and that alone, is the way to speed His appearing (3:12).

THE MOTIVES OF MINISTRY

Warm-up: 1 Peter 5:1–4

Be shepherds of God's flock that is under your care . . . as God wants you to be (1 Peter 5:2).

Persecution was in the air; Peter put it on the line: "It is hard for the righteous to be saved" (1 Peter 4:18); which means, among other things, that sooner or later, all of God's people will suffer.

Suffering sheep need a tender shepherd, which is why Peter appeals to his fellow-elders, saying, "tend God's flock under your care" (5:2).

However, tending injured sheep isn't always what it's cracked up to be. There's a lot of romantic nonsense attached to the role. The "joy of ministry," as some folks put it, may elude us. Certainly there are flashes of glory but mostly it's just hard, unsafe work.

What, then, will keep us going when the going gets tough? Certainly not that we're driven by need. A need, no matter how clamant, doesn't necessarily constitute a call.

Nor will we be sustained by some habit in our family (a "tradition of ministry," as they say), nor by some fleeting inclination to "go into full-time Christian service," which may come from any devil, disposition, or mood.

And certainly we should not be compelled by personal ambition. It can only consume us in the end.

Not even love for the sheep will keep us going. The sheep are sometimes insufferable. If it's only a love for sheep that constrains us, we'll end up hating them after a while.

It should go without saying that we're not motivated by money. Good shepherds are "not greedy for money, but eager to serve . . . " (5:2), like Chaucer's country parson who

Did not set his benefice to hire,
nor left his sheep encumbered in the mire,
And run to London, unto Sainte Paul's
To seeken him a chantery for souls,
Or with a brotherhood to be enrolled;
But dwelt a home, and kept well his fold
So that the wolf might make it not miscarry;
He was a shepherd and no mercenary.

If we're driven by money and upward mobility it will only harden our hearts in the end. As Jesus said, when "the *hired* hand . . . sees the wolf coming, he abandons the sheep and runs away. . . . The man runs away . . . and *cares nothing for the sheep*" (John 10:12–13, emphasis added).

And finally, as Peter continues, good shepherds aren't driven by a need to control. They don't "[lord] it over those entrusted to [them] but [are] examples to the flock" (5:3). Shepherding is not driving the sheep but leading them—setting the pace and showing them how.

No, the only sufficient motivation for us is the will of God: Good shepherds should care for God's sheep, "not under compulsion, but voluntarily, *according to the will of God"* (1 Peter 5:2 NASB, emphasis added). The important thing—the only thing that will sustain us for the long haul—is that we've been called and chosen. Doing His will is the only sure thing.

Let me say it again: Shepherding is hard work and most of the time it goes unrewarded. People forget to give thanks. But here, at the end of Peter's short paragraph on shepherding, is his bottom-line promise: "When the Chief Shepherd appears, you will receive the crown of glory that will never fade away " (5:4).

Hard times will come, but the Shepherd, under whose watchful eye we serve, knows our efforts and will reward us in time. Not at the end of the day, perhaps, or even at the end of our stay, but surely at the end of the age.

THE WORK OF GOD

Warm-up: John 6:25–59

*What must we do to do the works
God requires? (John 6:28).*

I have this recurrent nightmare in which I come to church to preach on Sunday morning and there's no one there! I'm ready to go, but the saints don't show. The children's ditty comes to my mind, "Here's the church, here's the steeple; open the door, but where are the people?"

It doesn't take a Daniel or a dream therapist to interpret the vision. It grows out of a gut-level conviction that everything around here depends on *me*. If I don't preach with power, if I don't produce, the saints will fade and the church will fold. *I* must do the work of God.

For example, there were those folks who came to Jesus and asked what they could do "to do the works God requires?" Good question, we say. But Jesus sets us straight: "The work of God is this: to *believe* in the one he has sent" (John 6:28–29, emphasis added).

What audacity—to think that any of us can do God's work. Who can do God's work but God? If it is to be done at all, it must be done by faith in Him.

God's work is never done by human effort. Our efforts in fact are ruinous. We rush about with devotion and gusto, getting in the way, like Abraham, who attempted to do God's work for Him and delayed the coming of the promised son several years. There's no wisdom or power in our own toil.

Numbers, planning, techniques, and methods are no good apart from God. The weapons we employ "are not the weapons of the world . . ." (2 Cor. 10:4). It is by *faith* that we fight. The old heroes "through faith conquered kingdoms, administered justice, and gained what was promised . . . shut the mouths of lions, quenched the fury of the flames, and escaped the edge of the sword." It was by faith that "weakness was turned to strength; and [men and women] became powerful in battle and routed foreign armies" (Heb. 11:33–34). All these great works were done by simple, relaxed people who believed in God. I must beware lest I work too hard.

Whatever we have to do, then—whether planning an outing for kindergartners, evangelizing a fraternity, or facing a firing squad—is done by faith. There is no other way to do the works of God.

And so, as I ponder on my dream, it's hard to escape the conclusion that there's a perverse sort of hypocrisy at work here: I speak and write about faith but deep down in my soul I must yet believe that everything depends upon me.

"Not to worry!" I tell myself. Growing my faith, like every other work, is a job for God! Belief is His gift to give (Eph. 2:8–9). And so I ask Him every day to increase my measure, praying, as Mother Teresa prayed, "Lord give me a vision of faith that Your work may be done."

BECOMING A LEGEND

Warm-up: Hebrews 11:1–40

*Faith is being sure of what we hope for
and certain of what we do not see (Heb. 11:1).*

Be honest now. Is there a flyfisher alive who never once wanted to become a legend; who never fantasized about walking into a fly shop and putting a hush on the assembled crowd? "That's old Double-Haul Dave," they would say with a nudge.

Unfortunately, it hasn't worked out that way for me. I've never achieved even that fifteen minutes of fame that Andy Warholl promised each of us. If, like Ogden Nash, one defines achievement as progress toward perfection, most of my progress has been in the other direction. If I am famous at all, it is for the number of times I've fallen into the South Fork of the Boise River instead of the number of fish I've taken out of it.

I did meet a legend once—a certain Polly Roseborough whom I chanced upon in a shop in Oregon. He autographed one of his books for me and gave me a fly that he had tied—one of his "fuzzy nymphs." It still hangs over my fly-tying table in a place of honor. No one else knows what it is, but it has special meaning for me: It represents my closest brush with a celebrity.

All of this set me to thinking about the stuff of which legends are made. Then I thought of some words in the book of Hebrews: "Faith is being sure of what we hope for and certain of what we do not see. This is what the ancients were commended for" (Heb. 11:1–2). Following this recipe we find a list of ingredients—men and women who became legends in their time. So who were these people and what did they do to become legends?

To make their long stories short, we're told in summary that they "conquered kingdoms, administered justice, and gained what was promised . . . shut the mouths of lions, quenched the fury of the flames, and escaped the edge of the sword . . . became powerful in battle and routed foreign armies" (11:33–34). Not bad for a bunch of ordinary people!

When we read about men and women in the Bible we should be aware that they're in our league. If they made something of themselves it's because there was another dynamic at work. The writer of Hebrews calls it *faith*.

Hebrews 11 isn't about people who believed things that were hard to believe. It's about men and women who were willing to do things that were hard to do. Abel offered an appropriate sacrifice and put his life on the line—because God asked him to; Enoch sought out God and began to walk with him when no one else would go along—because God asked him to; Noah began to build his embarrassing, monstrous supership miles from sea or stream, with no rain in sight—because God asked him to; Abraham left his home and his friends and moved to Canaan—because God asked him to. The list goes on.

In other words, faith doesn't begin in the intellect, but in the will. So we can begin to do what He is asking us to do. And when we do, we get His resources to carry on. I don't know if that means we'll ever become legends among our peers, but like those old-timers of faith, we'll become legendary in God's eyes. He never promised more or less.

And so the question for each of us is, "What is God now asking me to do?" for we all know in one way or another what He wants us to do. Perhaps the issue is withheld forgiveness, impurity of mind or body, or an act of kindness long delayed. Perhaps it's a ministry in which we're called to invest ourselves though the way seems weary and long. No one has to tell us what it is. We know.

As Jesus said, "Now that you know these things, you will be blessed if you do them" (John 13:17)

FINISHING STRONG

Warm-up: 2 Timothy 4:6–8

I have fought the good fight, I have finished the race, I have kept the faith (2 Tim. 4:7).

It occurs to me that it's good to have us older folks around. Otherwise, young people might forget that they too are getting old. We're harbingers of things to come; the prophets of everyone's destiny. Aging isn't just for the aged. It's the most common experience of all.

Since aging is inevitable, I'd just as soon get on with it. But I know some folks who don't want to get old. Like the problem of death, they wish someone would do something about it. Perhaps someone will. I read the other day that genetic engineers have already extended the life span of a single cell. It's possible that in the near future the deterioration of the remainder of our parts can be arrested somewhat. Perhaps a few years can be added to our lives.

Yet the question that comes to me is whether those extra years will be worth living. If not, we're no better off than Aurora, the mythical Roman, who asked the gods for eternal life and got it, but just kept getting older. Believe me, there's nothing inherently good about just getting old.

There are two ways to view the aging process: We can dread it, or we can view it with faith, believing that old age can be "good old age" as the Old Testament puts it.

The world is constantly telling us in one way or another that the youthful years are the good years. The earlier days are those in which we find excitement, adventure, and worth—"the days of wine and roses."

But I can't agree. I have to say, as Jesus' friends did at the wedding in Cana, that He saves the best wine until the last. The Lord takes these later years of our lives, touches them with unsurpassing fragrance, and turns them into fine wine.

I think of Robert Browning's lines:

Grow old along with me,
    The best is yet to be,
The last of life
    For which the first was made.

Take my friend Ray. Like Enoch, he's been walking with the Lord for a long, long time and growing from "faith to faith," as Paul would say. Like Caleb at eighty and Abraham at ninety he's more inclined than ever before to lean on God. That nearness has rubbed off on him: I now see more of God's presence in Ray than ever before. What an impact he's making!

His walk with God has kept him in the thick of things. With the old veteran of Psalm 71, even when "old and gray," he has "[declared God's] power to the next generation, [his] might to all who are to come" (71:18).

He's one of the few older men I know who's still on the cutting edge. I hope I have half his vitality and vision when I get to be his age.

I've learned from him that aging doesn't have to be

dying. It can be growing, maturing, serving, ministering, moving with anticipation toward that hour when I say with the apostle Paul, "The time has come for my departure. I have fought the good fight, I have *finished* the race, I have kept the faith" (2 Tim. 4:6–7, emphasis added).

Never give up! One is never too old to be fruitful. "Age is not decay; it is ripening, the swelling of the fresh life within" (George MacDonald). No one has ever out-lived the power of God.

Other Discovery House material that will feed your soul with the Word of God:

My Utmost for His Highest
by *Oswald Chambers*

The classic devotional bestseller. These powerful words will refresh those who need encouragement, brighten the way of those in difficulty, and strengthen personal relationships with Christ. A book to use every day for the rest of your life. *An audio cassette edition is also available.*

Broken Things: *Why We Suffer*
by *M. R. De Haan, M. D.*

To those seeking reasons for their suffering and disappointments, this book offers hope and peace through the healing principles of God's Word.

What Jesus Said About Successful Living:
Principles from the Sermon on the Mount
by *Haddon W. Robinson*

A powerful application of the Sermon on the Mount principles as the path to true happiness. The author illustrates how believers can pray wholeheartedly, serve devotedly, and trust completely.

The Strength of a Man: *Encouragement for Today*
by *David Roper*

Fifty short, easy-to-read chapters that explore topics such as money, failure, humility, fear, and prayer. A biblical look at true manhood.

Daniel: *God's Man in a Secular Society*
by *Donald K. Campbell*

Intriguing, contemporary perspective and helpful application of the prophecies in Daniel. A call to radical dependence on God.

Waiting for the Second Coming: *Studies in Thessalonians*
by *Ray Stedman*
Dr. Stedman provides new insight for today's problems and offers future hope in the certainty of Christ's return. Full of encouragement for world-weary believers.

The Parables: *Understanding What Jesus Meant*
by *Gary Inrig*
The author challenges us to sit at Jesus' feet and listen to these twelve wonderful stories as though we were hearing them for the first time.

Love Without Shame: *Sexuality in Biblical Perspective*
by *David Wyrtzen*
A compelling and uplifting "theology of sexuality." Important reading for leaders responsible for premarital and marriage counseling.

Prophecy for Today: *God's Purpose and Plan for Our Future*
by *J. Dwight Pentecost*
The great themes of prophecy are presented in popular, nontechnical language.

The following resources are part of the Discovery Interactive Bible Study series, a video curriculum complete with leader's guide and study booklets for your class:

How Can I Feel Good About Myself?
Is self-esteem merely a humanistic issue? What about the Bible and the subject of self-esteem? These lessons are designed to help you teach the biblical perspective on this issue.

Where Can We Find Comfort?

Where can damaged souls find a place to renew faith, hope, and love in the midst of pain? These lessons answer this and other questions through interactive teaching sessions.

Who Needs the Church?

This series answers the questions people are asking about the relevance of the church for today's world.

Order from your favorite bookstore or from:

DISCOVERY HOUSE PUBLISHERS
Box 3566
Grand Rapids, MI 49501
Call toll-free: 1-800-283-8333

Discoveries: *A Letter for Pastors from Radio Bible Class*

You may also wish to be placed on the mailing list for the free Radio Bible Class newsletter called *Discoveries*. The newsletter is designed by pastors for pastors and includes a wealth of current illustrations, insights, and other important information. To receive your copy of *Discoveries*, simply send your name, church name, and address to:

RADIO BIBLE CLASS
Grand Rapids, MI 49555-0001
Call toll-free: 1-800-950-7221